Seanchas na Midhe

A SELECTION OF LECTURES

MAIGHRÉAD UÍ CHONMHIDHE

EDITED BY

MÉADHBH NÍ CHONMHIDHE PISKORSKA

AND

MÁIRE BRÜCK

i

First published in 2009 by

Foilsitheoirí an Mhóta.

First Edition.

Book design by andrew@andrewbruck.com

The painting on the cover, Mornington Tower, oil on canvas by Maighréad
Uí Chonmhidhe is reproduced by kind permission of Meath County Council.

A catalogue record for this book is available from the British Library.

ISBN 978-0-9561744-0-6

Printed by Ross Print Services, Greystones, County Wicklow. Tel: 01 287 6612

Maighréad Uí Chonmhidhe
(Margaret Conway)

Contents

Reamhra

Tá saothar Mhaighréad Uí Chonmhidhe i réimse cultúrtha agus staire áitiúil, a ullmhu ag a h-inion Meadhbh, go príomha an t-ábhar a foilsíodh sa *Meath Chronicle*, dar teideal *Towards a History of Meath* agus *A Parish History Of Meath*, agus léachtaí a thug sí do chomhaltaí de Bhantracht na Tuaithe, de Mhacra na Tuaithe, do Chumann Seandálaíochta agus Staire na Mí, agus ag ócáidí ar nós Cuimhneacháin an Athar Eoin Ó Gramhnaigh, agus Féile na Bóinne.

Bhí sé i gceist aici leagan den ábhar a chur le chéile i bhfoirm leabhar. Chuir sí roimpi an stair a thabhairt chun solais as na comharthaí a rinne an duine ar thalamh na Mí leis na cianta fada – caisleáin agus botháin, fothracha séipéil is Eaglaise, monarchana agus tithe nua aimsire.

Ba thrua dar lei go mbeadh an aos óg a bhfuil na mílte blian de shaothar an duine mar oidhre aca dall ar an saidhbhreas sin a thugann blas dúinn ar ár nduthaigh féin. Is go deonach a rinne sí an obair mar mhaithe le daoine a spreagadh le a n-oidhreacht teanga agus béascna a aithint agus a cheiliúradh agus is mar sin a ghlac sí páirt ins na coistí cultúrtha sa chontae – Conradh na Gaeilge, an Coiste Gairm Oideachais, agus an Coiste Leabharlanna ina measc.

Ba é guí a fear céile Tomás go gcuirfí an t-ábhar seo ar fáil do ghlún óg na Mí.

Foreword

The work of Margaret Conway (1898-1974), local historian, writer and lecturer, comprises articles contributed over many years to the Meath Chronicle, together with lectures given under various auspices – Macra na Tuaithe, the Irish Countrywomen's Association, The Meath Archaeological and Historical Society, The Boyne Festival, The O Growney Memorial lecture – and those given to students in schools and Farm Schools.

They date from 1939 (a lecture on Oliver Goldsmith) to her last public lecture on Francis Ledwidge on the occasion of the launch of Alice Curtayne's biography in 1974.

The Meath County Library welcomed the opportunity to assist in the preparation of the Meath Chronicle series for inclusion on its web site, and its local history and web site specialists have brought the work to its final stages. The unpublished material is being edited by Meadhbh who intends to make it available to a new generation, also on a web site. In the meantime some examples of her lectures are selected here for family and friends as a reminder of her devotion to our local county, and of her love of history and literature.

We also reprint here Meadhbh's commemorative essay on Margaret Conway's key role in the re-birth of the Meath Archaeological and Historical Society and as founding editor of its scholarly journal *Ríocht na Midhe,* published in 2005 on the 50th anniversary of the journal's inception. *Ríocht na Midhe*, which Margaret Conway edited for its first 12 years, is her enduring legacy in the wider world of academic learning.

The eminent historian Professor Alfred P. Smyth, in his *Faith, Famine and Fatherland in the Nineteenth Century Irish Midlands* (Dublin: Four Courts Press 1992), describes it in his bibliography as 'an essential point of departure for all historians working on Meath and Westmeath.' He writes: '*Ríocht na Midhe, Records of the Meath Archaeological Society*, beginning with Vol. 1 in 1955 and continuing to the present, provides an invaluable series of articles on all matters relating to Meath and Westmeath prehistory, medieval archaeology and history, as well as to the modern history and folklore of the region.' Margaret Conway's own contributions are listed in the *Ríocht na Midhe* Author Index (to be found on the Society's web site), and may be read in full in the journal itself in some local and university libraries.

Margaret Conway, founding editor of Ríocht na Midhe.

Reprinted (abridged) by kind permission of the Editor
from *Ríocht na Midhe* Volume 16, 2005, 194-211.

Ríocht na Midhe, with this edition celebrates 50 years of publication. By any standards *Ríocht na Midhe* is a remarkable achievement and a tribute to the various editors, to the Council and membership of the society over the years, and to the people of the ancient kingdom of Meath who have appreciated and supported it.

My mother, Mrs Margaret Conway, was its first editor from 1955 up to 1967, and Secretary of Meath Archaeological and Historical Society from 1937 to 1962. My mother's papers include some which relate to the Meath Archaeological and Historical Society of the time. It is an honour for me to have been asked to describe the character of its early years and tell something of the people associated with it: in this I have drawn on my recollections and those of other members of the family, and I have spoken to families and acquaintances of some of the early members.

The landscape of the ancient kingdom of Meath draws everyone of us into an artistic engagement with its powerful and magical presence: 'For from the days when man first reached our island and made his way along the rivers, through the centuries when High Kings ruled from Tara, during the later invasions, in the ebb and flow of plantation and absorption, conquest and resurgence, every period in the history of Ireland has left its traces in the great plain of the Ancient Kingdom of Meath' (from our first number). I do not think it fanciful to suggest that this long history of habitation is the primary life force of the Society, but it took the 'enquiring mind and the mission to take care of ancient lore' of Father R. R. Callary, *Ardollamh re Seanchas*, to create the organisation and subsequently his inspiration and tenacity to ensure the publication and the continuation of these latter-day annals of the kingdom.

My earliest memory of Father Callary goes back to the thirties, and to his lectures in the open air on some hillside when we children heard for the first time of the mysterious Bronze Age, while at the same time chasing each other round forts and ruined walls.

My warmest recollections are of his frequent visits to us when we went to live in Moattown, after my father's retirement in 1951. This would also have been a time of intense work on the preparation for the first edition of the journal, *Ríocht na Midhe*. Fr Callary used to arrive in the early afternoon on Sundays from Ballinabrackey where he was parish priest. He never could be persuaded to have lunch with us – we called it dinner in those days – as he would just have finished breakfast after his Mass duties, but he would have a cup of tea. I remember him as a gentle person with what I now call old-world manners, and indeed the same code dictated that no one would dream of letting it be known that the family dinner was ready, so he would feel at home for as long as he wished to stay. The conversation was often about something he was planning for the Society. As President he would have been the one responsible for ensuring the flow of activity – and that the activity was maintained. He himself was among the most prolific; he gave many lectures to the renewed society of the late thirties – *The Kingdom of Meath* (1937), *The Graves of Loughcrew, Tara,* and *The History and Antiquities of Trim* (all in 1938), and he contributed to the first four editions of *Ríocht,* in the Fifties.

The Meath Archaeological and Historical Society of 1937 was a reincarnation of the one founded in 1919 at a General Meeting on 25 August 1919 in St Mary's Hall, Mullingar, at which Father Paul Walsh was elected President and Father Callary was elected Secretary and Treasurer. He maintained his commitment to the Society, despite time spent abroad because of his health, through the long years of difficulty caused by the unsettled state of the country. It was through him that the 1918-19 Society would live on in spirit, in unbroken succession, up to the reconstitution of the Society in 1937, when he was elected President and Fr Walsh became vice-president for Westmeath.

My mother, Margaret Conway, was Secretary of the Meath Archaeological and Historical Society from 1937 for 25 years, and first editor of *Ríocht* (1955) until 1967. She was a native of Co. Louth, and a Meath woman by adoption rather than by birth, who married into an old Meath family. She came to teach in Coolronan in 1923 and remained there during her entire working life. She was active in the public life of the county and served on the Vocational Education Committee and on the Library Committee, as well on many voluntary committees, including *Conradh na Gaeilge.* She was in a sense a sage called upon to add her wisdom and experience to whatever new movement was being put in train.

Her presence as Secretary was therefore inevitable, a source of strength as all-pervasive as the landscape, and as elusive. She was *ildánach* – gifted in many ways. She was artistic and always had a sketch book in hand. I remember a perfect pen and ink drawing of Bective Abbey she made when she brought us to see it as children, and some of her paintings are in the collection of Meath County Council; she it was who designed the original cover for *Ríocht na Midhe,* redolent of the period. She wrote fluently and with style; she had a sense of history, and she had the capacity to draw together ideas from various sources and convey them with clarity; she was intelligent and imaginative. But over and above these gifts was her generosity of spirit. She was modest about herself and was totally devoid of vanity. She was serene and comfortable in her personality and so seemed to have all the time in the world for whatever was going on at any particular moment. With my father, the household was a welcoming one. She was herself a historian although she would make no claims to be such; she was a very skilled researcher. I have been astounded at the breadth and extent of her work, and by her respect for the knowledge stored in the living tradition. She was competent and efficient in the basic administrative tasks. She kept the records of the Society, convened meetings, wrote detailed reports of Council meetings. The annual reports were comprehensive and she was aware of their function as raw material for the Society's history; at crucial moments she summarised the story of the Society to date, incorporating those parts from the earlier days as she learned of them. I have some of these reports in the original, in her strong legible hand, with few if any corrections. She was a clear thinker, and as Boileau the French stylist said, what is clearly thought, can be clearly expressed. This ability stood her in good stead in her role as editor of the journal. She could give context and form to an article offered for *Ríocht* with a simple phrase or a sentence, and ironed out awkward expression with a minimum of alteration.

A strong ally in this work was Mrs McGurl (née McNevin). Her contribution to the Society over many years and as Assistant Editor for the first edition of *Ríocht na Midhe* was invaluable; she brought to it her scholarship and her professional skills as a librarian. Mary Kate McNevin had a Master's degree from U.C.D. and spent some time in Bonn on a travelling studentship under the direction of that great Celtic scholar Rudolf Thurneyesen (1857-1940). Karl Wurm, who was a colleague of my late brother-in-law when they both worked in Potsdam Observatory, remembered the 'two lovely Irish girls' – the other was Kathleen Mulchrone, late Professor of Old Irish at U.C.G., who were fellow students in Bonn.

M.K. McNevin married Seán McGurl in 1944. She still is remembered in librarian circles as a very able and formidable woman, one of the group of pioneer librarians in the early days of the Public Library service, which had to withstand various pressures and at times outright hostility. She was conscientious and uncompromising in her own standards, but I remember her as enjoying company during the Christmas visits to our house, herself and Seán and whoever else might be there. Her account of her association with the Meath Archaeological and Historical Society is typical of her wry sense of humour and of her conscientious approach to work. She tells us in an article in the *Irish Library Bulletin* that her interest in archaeology was acquired because of her membership of the Society which she joined as part of a librarian's work 'which must spread its tentacles towards all the cultural movements in the locality... I could not profess any enthusiasm for this society at the start and just looked on the whole county as an incongruous mass of monuments to such people as Wellington and then Round Towers and ruins... but the society bred in me a respect for the genuine antiquities.' The landscape had once more asserted its power.

The renewed Society got under way in 1937. At the first meeting Rev. P. Mulvany (Chairman) explained that 'a good deal of preparation has been made by a small committee of workers to establish the Society in Meath. Father Callary has been acting as Chairman and Mrs Conway as Secretary.'

A provisional committee set about its work with energy, meeting frequently to plan and carry out various activities and negotiating with the Board of Works for the preservation and restoration of certain ancient churches in the area – Portlomman, Inchmore, Kilpatrick, Dunboden and Ballyboggan. They planned a survey of the 'lesser known antiquities of the district and the collection of oral tradition in relation to them.' A member was put in charge of each barony, and the public was asked to contribute material, however small. The report for 1938 makes a reference to the work of the schools for the Folklore Society as a source; it lists the outings and lectures which the provisional council had arranged – Father Callary delivered addresses at Tara and Loughcrew, and Father Gibbons one at Fore. Father Gibbons' lecture is remembered by the writer of an obituary tribute to him in the *Meath Chronicle* (9 December 1939) 'who had last met him in his own well loved Fore, where he lectured on the ruins in the summer of 1938.'

Further lectures were by Father Callary on 'The History and Antiquities of Trim', Father Paul Walsh on 'The History of the Mageoghan Chiefs from the 13th to the 17th Century' and Ven. Archdeacon Healy on 'Some Stories of Ancient Kells'. Archdeacon Healy was a scholar and his two volume *History of the Diocese of Meath* (1908), a valuable reference work, and his earlier *The Ancient*

Irish Church (1895) are among his publications. He was rector of
Kells from 1887 to 1917 and Archdeacon of Meath from 1914 to
1928. My mother gave a talk, 'Goldsmith Country', on 19 August
1939, in which various strands of history and literature are brought
together. She identifies the Village Schoolmaster in *The Deserted
Village* as Paddy or Thomas Byrne, a poet and Gaelic scholar who
translated Virgil into Irish, and she makes the connection with
Turlough O Carolan. The vote of thanks was by Dr Beryl Moore,
Athboy, seconded by Fr Callary. Also present were M.K. McNevin,
Meath County Librarian, Mr Joe Conway N.T., Raharney and Seán
MacNamidhe. These details I gleaned from a surviving copy of the
booklet made available by *The Westmeath Examiner*.

Society records in 1939 indicate a significant lapse in progress.
'The unfortunate conditions prevailing since the autumn which
prevented the Society from carrying out the programme of lectures
to be held in co-operation with the Meath Vocational Education
Committee' probably arose from the outbreak of war in September
1939 and advent of petrol rationing, allowing only eight gallons
monthly for a small car, which was introduced in the beginning of
October. However during 1939 Harold Leask, Inspector of Ancient
Monuments, gave a lecture with lantern slides on the Architecture
in the Kingdom of Meath from the beginning of the Christian
Period to the seventeenth Century. A major success for the Society
was its persuasion of Meath County Council to adopt the Ancient
Monuments Act and to appoint an Advisory Committee. The
members of the Committree were Seán McGurl, Chairman of the
Meath Co. Council, Mr E. Duffy, BE., Meath County Surveyor and
three members of the Society: Rev. R.R. Callary, Rev. J. Mooney
C.C. and D.F.O. Sullivan.

Seán McGurl's chairmanship of the Advisory Council was a good
omen for the Society. Seán lived in Kildalkey and cycled everywhere
including the trek to the monthly meetings of the board of
Mullingar Mental Hospital, of which he was also a member. He

often called to us on his way to or from these meetings. Seán had the face of a man who more often smiled than frowned; he was a most courteous man, a courtesy he extended quite naturally to children. He kept a child's enthusiasm for life but as a councillor he could be tough and decisive. He remained as Chairman of Meath County Council up to 1942. Seán McGurl was later to be the Hon. Treasurer of the Society but at this time the Provisional Council did not have a named treasurer – so my mother gives summary accounts in each of these reports. The membership on 31 December 1938 totalled forty-two; subscriptions received totalled £18 and the balance to the credit of the society is nine pounds one shilling and sixpence. In 1939 they gained 12 new members, giving 58 in all.

In 1950 a public meeting was arranged and the Society entered on a programme of activities with the object of re-awakening public interest in its work. Winter lectures were given in Trim, An Uaimh and Kells and out-door talks at Tara, Killeen, Loughcrew and other places. Father Callary and Seán MacNamidhe contributed a series of articles to *The Meath Chronicle.*

Margaret Conway wrote a comprehensive report arising from that meeting dated June 1954 which summarises the main rules, sketches the history, gives the names of the 1937 council members (she typically omits her own name), lists the activities and their coverage in the three papers, *The Meath Chronicle*, *The Westmeath Examiner* and *The Drogheda Independent*, and notes the effects of wartime shortages in bringing public lectures and outings to an end. She notes the valuable work of collecting done by individual members: Mr. D.F. O'Sullivan is singled out. She lists the Society's achievements: the adoption of the Ancient Monuments Acts by the County Council and the recent acquisition of part of the hill of Tara through The Advisory Committee acting with Meath County Council. The report goes on: 'But one of the most important objects of the Society has not yet been attempted – namely the publication of a journal. There is enough material, all that is lacking is the funds

– there is £27 in hand but we would need £100 to be able to publish a journal. Members are therefore requested to pay their 1955 subscriptions in advance.'

At the Trim meeting the former Council were empowered to act. The members were: Father Callary; Mr S. McGurl, Hon Treasurer; Mrs M. Conway, Hon. Sec; Mrs S. McGurl, Mr Sean MacNamidhe and Mr Mathew Reilly. An editorial sub-committee was appointed: Fr Callary, Mrs McGurl, Mrs Hickey, Mr Hussey of *The Drogheda Independent*, Mr O'Reilly, Mr MacNamidhe and Mr Conway.

By January 1955, the Society had 74 members, and the title was chosen: *Ríocht na Midhe, records of the Meath Archaeological and Historical Society;* the material was collected and 'of a high standard, and sufficiently varied to interest the general reader as well as the specialist and the committee are working on the illustrations.'

My mother's voluminous papers yield up much additional information. We learn how the passage on the title page of the journal, taken from *Tecosca Cormaic, Cormac's Instructions* came to be chosen. My mother asked Rev. W.F. Conlon, President of the Classical School in Navan, to peruse the Triads or the like to find a suitable passage to serve as a motto for the journal. He replied on the 3 March 1955: 'Have skimmed the Triads and have found nothing very apposite. I enclose a passage from Teagasc Chormaic which I thought might be adaptable to your purpose.'

One of the letters of Pádraig Ó hUiginn is dated 6 January 1955 – round about the time the journal was being prepared. It is in his distinctive Gaelic script:

I dtaoibh an 'Record' agus airgead an Chumainn: Éist leis seo! Mise a thosnuigh Feis Mhuighe Bhreagha ag Domhnach Seachnaill ins na blianta 1925 -1945... Nuair d'fhág mise an ceantar sin i 1945, níor cuireadh aon t-suim i bhFeis ó shoin...

Tá suas le £30 punt sa gciste fós… b'fhearr an t-airgead sin a chur ar fail i gcóir Irise nó "Record" don Chumann le Arsaíocta mar gurab é rud is goire do obair Feise é sa gceantar.

This touching gesture shows us Pádraig Ó hUiginn suggesting that the dormant funds of the Feis Committee be transferred to the Society. He proposes that my mother should request Dr Conway (Ratoath), Vice Chair, to convene a Feis committee meeting to deal with the matter. Pádraig Ó hUiginn was active in the lead up to the publication of the journal. I remember him very well, and his house in Summerhill, and years later I worked with his grand-daughter in RTE. He was born in 1885 in Doon, Roscahill, in the parish of Kilannin, Co. Galway. Irish was at that time the spoken language of the district. After leaving the primary school he attended the Irish college ag Tuar Mhic Éadaigh. These Irish colleges attracted students of all ages – Pokorny and Kuno Meyer were students a decade later – and were a source of rich cultural experience. Pádraig went on to teach Irish in Glasgow and to study Scots Gaelic. He came to Co. Meath as 'múinteoir taistil' travelling all over on his bicycle. He was a man of broad interest and was familiar with astronomy, history, archaeology and folklore. He spent much of his free time visiting notable places throughout Co. Meath and he considered Meath to be the most historically interesting county of all. He enjoyed talking to old people about traditional customs, and finding out the origins and meanings of names of places, townlands and parishes. He was an expert on Ambrose O'Higgins of Brazil and contributed pieces to early numbers of *Ríocht na Midhe*.

The Society papers kept by my mother include just one letter from Seán MacNamidhe, dated 18-2-'55, addressed from 45 Cannon Row. He encloses an article for *Ríocht* and says he is not too well since October '54, but is improving. He asks if she would give a title to the article but he then suggests a title himself: 'Some notes on Navan, Ancient and Modern,' which my mother used. This is a most attractive piece and at a distance of 50 years it records traditions and conveys a feel for the town now no longer current.

Seán MacNamidhe deserves a full biography to do proper justice to a man who endured his share of injustice. Such a biography would highlight his life of dedication to the service of the public, his contributions to the original *Sinn Féin* paper founded in Co. Meath, his attempts to preserve and honour the graves of the poor people who died in the workhouses during the Great Famine, his contribution to education in the county and most important in this context, his crucial role in sustaining with Father Callary the Meath Archaeological and Historic Society through the difficult years.

Margaret Conway's papers include several letters from Father John Brady, who was Diocesan Historian and a scholar of high standing. His article 'The first Patrician Church Site -– a suggested identification' reveals much of the quality of the man himself: it is scholarly and presents a challenge to eminent predecessors but without any trace of arrogance. He contributed an article to every number of the journal until his death in 1963, and the Society has paid due tribute to him in assembling a bibliography of his articles.

I remember one of the occasions I met him: he was coming with my mother over to the car after she had called on him at home. He lived at the family home and they had a public house in Dunboyne. I had the impression that he was a shy person and that his health was never robust. My mother had the highest regard for him. The following extract from the obituary she wrote for him in *Ríocht na Midhe* is from the heart: 'Others more able than I am have paid tribute to his work. I can only recall here his great kindness to me when, as editor of your records I appealed to him out of my ignorance and inexperience, and he gave me always without a trace of condescension, the advice and criticism of a very great man who was also a simple and sincere friend.' I think that my mother asked for Fr Brady's advice on specialist articles that she judged to be outside her area of competence, especially with new contributors whose credentials were obscure.

Among the most active members of the Society was R.F.G. Adams, F.R.S.A.I. He was constantly engaged in meticulous field work and in stimulating the interest of local people in the monuments of their countryside. I can see him in my mind's eye, a man of commanding appearance, standing on a very slight height, pointing out features of the landscape and I remember most clearly his delight in articulating the word 'moteen' (a small moat – a feature of the landscape in the Fore district) pausing after the first vowel to pronounce the following syllable *con brio* as if to show how well he had mastered the slender *t/k* of the Meath-Westmeath dialect of Hiberno-English. He wrote to my mother regularly in advance of council meetings from Rockview, Delvin (Co. Westmeath) usually proposing a choice of themes for papers, and suggesting locations and topics for outings or lectures.

The link with the National Museum, noted in the foreword to the first number of the journal was maintained. The museum supplied lists of acquisitions from the district, and members drew the Museum's attention to sites of possible interest. The professional staff, Breandán Ó Riordáin, Nell Prendergast and Etienne Rynne, made occasional contributions to *Ríocht,* often at my mother's request. There is quite a correspondence with Dr Lucas and it exemplifies the cross over between my mother's work with the Meath Archaeological Society and her articles for *The Meath Chronicle* which she wrote from 1956 to 1961. These articles gave her the opportunity to collect memories and information about people and places, craft and tradition. She gave assistance to Dr Lucas in his study of furze which was the subject of his doctorate.

A significant source of material for the journal was Mathew Reilly, who was a mine of information. He was on the Council in 1937 and contributed to the early numbers of *Ríocht*. He was a handsome man with a shock of greying hair and he was one of the O Reillys of Williamstown, descendants of an old Irish family. In his earlier years he spent time in Argentina in connection with the cattle trade. He was a studious man and he had a considerable library of scholarly and antiquarian books. He was a Teachta Dála from 1927 to 1954. I remember meeting him along the quays in the early fifties perusing the various street bookstalls, in the intervals of Dáil business.

Dr Moran was asked if he would be willing to succeed Fr Callary as President. Dr Wm Moran was Vice-President for Offaly, and while he is not listed as a member of the council of 1919, nor of the Society in 1937, by 1955 he was a full member and is singled out for special mention, as already noted, in the report of January 21, 1955.

Dr Moran wrote:

I could not possibly take on the presidency or attend meetings of Council. I will be 74 in March and am feeling accordingly. A priest as president would probably hold the society together better than a lay person. Of those you mention, Fr Gilsenan or Fr Shaw would be very suitable...

Fr Shaw would be willing to travel to meetings and in any case he has a phone now. [Note that the telephone is still a rarity.]

A further letter from Dr Moran on 21 February 1961 goes as follows:

I am afraid Fr Shaw cannot be persuaded to step into the gap... Unless you can get some curate who is fairly centrally situated to step into the breach, I think we shall have to ask Mr Adams, the only one, at least among the men, who is enthusiastic. The only alternative would be to get a lady to take the job. The Society has had an uphill struggle, and is not yet secure...

The lady in question was Mrs McGurl. It is more than likely that my mother spoke to her about taking on the presidency after a Library Committee Meeting. In any event the matter is now resolved as we see from Dr Moran's letter (21 February 1961):

I am glad you have got Mrs McGurl to agree to accept nomination. I was beginning to fear that the society would lapse into the moribund condition in which it was for so many years. It is no good to have a president that is not alive, active and enthusiastic for the work of the Society. If a priest with these qualifications were available, I think he would be the wise choice. In the absence of one, a layperson, man or woman with the qualifications should be elected.

These remarks have to be read bearing in mind that a journal for 'The Ancient Kingdom of Meath' was initially proposed by the great scholar Father Paul Walsh and his friend the first president, Father Callary. Clergymen of all denominations were prominent in its development – Canon Rowland Athey, Canon Ellison, Archdeacon Healy, Father Gibbons and Father John Brady, and including Mgr John Hanly (Sean Ó hÁinle), currently parish priest of Laytown, who contributed to the last two numbers edited by my mother. Many of them had university degrees in the Humanities, and had more control over their working hours than people in paid employment.

Mrs McGurl was a worthy choice for the presidency. She brought to the task all the talents at her disposal, and a steadfast commitment. She held the presidency for the full term. Her successor as President was Dr Beryl Moore, who was proposed by my mother, Mrs Margaret Conway, at the Annual General Meeting held in Slane on Thursday 7 March 1968. At that meeting she also proposed Mr Michael Ward as editor to succeed herself. He was succeeded in 1971 by Fr Gerald Rice. Fr Joe Paul Kelly was already Honorary Secretary, a post he filled with distinction and with the exuberance he brought to all his activity.

A brief roll call of other women who contributed to the history of the Society and the journal includes Mrs Hickey, already given her place of honour, and we recall with affection her beautiful *'I'll send my love along the Boyne';* Beryl Moore, the third president who contributed to several editions of *Ríocht* from her extensive surveys, in particular of graveyards, and was also watchful that no untoward development desecrated these holy places; Mrs Vandeleur, who was secretary of the Killucan branch of the Society; and Hanna Fitzsimons who held the fort in the interval between Father Callary's acceptance of the Life Presidency and the election of Mrs McGurl. Finally there was Helen Roe, a distinguished scholar and the first woman President of the Royal Society of Antiquaries of Ireland. Helen Roe was commissioned by the Society to write the *High Crosses of Kells* – quite a courageous undertaking. Her next work for the Society was to document the mediaeval fonts of County Meath, some of which were scattered among ruined churches in remote places. My mother thought it prudent to have one or other of my brothers, Ultan or Loman, come with them to help them over hedges and ditches; both men now remember these days with affection and as not lacking in adventure.

In a letter to my mother, Helen Roe describes a newly-formed historical society in the Midlands as being 'full of aimless and formless good will' and here comes a tribute to my mother – 'I do not think it will long survive unless the willing horse is discovered somewhere. As you full well know you're it [for Meath] and the grey mare too!'

She was one of many who received hospitality from my father and mother. Indeed our house continued to be a focal point for many of the Society's guests. Professor Patrick McBride, of University College Dublin, brought a Spanish de Lacy, a descendant of the Wild Geese, to our house. He wrote in March 1953 thanking us for the hospitality and in particular Eithne for the supper she provided. Professor McBride again contacted my mother in 1957, and she arranged to have a civic reception accorded by the Urban District Council of an Uaimh to His Excellency, Lt-Gen. Alfredo Kindelan y Duano on July 14 1957, whose direct ancestor, Ultan Kindelan, left

Ballinakill for Spain in 1673. Father Callary and she represented the Society at this occasion.

I have recalled but a few of these early members. They were a remarkable group of people, who had seen the birth of a new nation and sought to enrich their knowledge of the countryside around them, which for them was the focus of their patriotism. For many of them Irish was their language of adoption, but whatever might have been their experience in those earlier turbulent years of the new state, the Society drew people together in a common project "to preserve, examine, publish and illustrate the antiquities, records and traditions connected with the territory." They retained the commitment to the objects of the Society through difficult years and finally achieved the goal of publishing a journal – of a standard that has ensured its survival for half a century.

After the passage of 50 years, I can best pay tribute to these pioneers by adapting the poem by Horace quoted by Father Callary in the first number of the journal in relation to County Meath's richly historic and very beautiful landscape to include their work also:

(They) have raised a monument more lasting than bronze,
More lofty than the Pyramids,
Which neither biting frost, nor raging north wind,
Neither the countless cycles of the years
Nor flight of time can bring to ruin.
(They) will not altogether die,
And a great part of them shall escape the hands of death.

Méadhbh Ni Chonmhidhe Piskorska

Place Names

Extract from a talk in 1956 in An Uaimh to the Irish
Countrywomen's Association. It is one of many on
the popular theme of place names and local history
delivered to various groups in various locations for
which manuscript notes are preserved. These places
include Kilmainham Wood, Lobinstown, Oldcastle,
Dunboyne, Robinstown and Ardee.

The interpretation of Irish place names is a highly specialised subject: to attempt it at all one would need a knowledge of the Irish language, not only as it is spoken and written today, but as it was spoken and written in medieval and ancient times; a similar knowledge of the English language since the time when that language began to be used here; acquaintance with the laws governing changes in the pronunciation of various sounds, and ability to read the oldest manuscripts extant.

Very few people therefore are competent to speak with authority on the subject, but that does not mean that it is one in which we cannot all be interested. Many names are quite readily intelligible to anyone with an ordinary working knowledge of the Irish language, and for many more the spade work has been done for us by such painstaking experts as Donovan, Joyce, O Curry and others.

We may take it, I think, as an axiom that every name had a meaning when it was first used; a meaning readily intelligible to everyone. We ourselves name places around us from some obvious feature; the white walls, the crooked turn, the five lamps, the railway bridge and so on, and we often add the name of the people who live near the place Carey's crossroads, Joyce's wood etc. This is exactly what happened from the beginning. The physical features are obvious sources of names – hills, glens, lakes and so on.

Sliabh, the Irish for a mountain is found all over Ireland, and is represented here by the lovely name of Sliabh Breagh in County Louth, and Sliabh Gullian on the Louth Armagh border, where the pronunciation is Sli' Guillian, an example of the tendency to drop altogether the sound of *bh*. Joyce gives the latter part as holly, but some give it as a person's name (the famous smith).

Cnoc the modern Irish for a hill is anglicised as Knock with the *K* silent or as Crock with the plural Crick. This latter is very common in North Meath and Louth. The Crickawee – the yellow hills, the Crockán the little hill, as names of fields.

Drom, literally a back, is very common also for a hill: Dromconra = Conra's hill, the Drommin, the little hill, Drumcar, the hill or ridge of the weir (Cora), Drumard, the high ridge, and Dromin which Joyce makes the same as Drommin, though it seems unlikely that the *in* would be accented in that case, Druim Samhraidh – anglicised as Summerhill... Summerhill in Co. Meath is Cnoc an Línsigh, and the Summerhill in Donegal is Cnoc an tSamhraidh.

Magh, a plain, naturally occurs very frequently in this part of the country. Near Summerhill in Meath there is a district known simply as The Moy where the English 'The' comes before the pure Irish word and gives us 'The plain.' Moynalty is the plain of the flocks, Moyvore, the great plain, Moyvalley, the plain of the roadway: bealach is a way.

The use of the article 'The' in The Naul on the Meath – Dublin border is curious. The Irish name is An Aill = the cliff (two words). In course of time the *n* got attached and English speakers put in a second article 'The' to give The Naul.

Another form of Magh is Machaire which gives us Magheracloon, the plain of the meadow. *Cluain* itself is very common. It is often shortened to *Clon* in this part of the country so we have Clonard, Iorard's meadow, Clonkeen, the gentle or soft meadow (the name of a Barony in Louth), Clongill, the foreigner's meadow (Gall), Clonduff, Cloneycavan, Cloneylogan, Clonmore and countless others.

Loch a lake or pool is too obvious to need mention. Loughfea, the old Shirley demesne near Carrickmacross is the Lake of the Bullrushes, and Carrick itself is of course a rock. *Machaire* and *Ros*, a woody promontory. We have several Rosses: Rosnaree and Rosmeen, the fine shrubbery, in Meath. *Carraig Leice* in North Meath is the Rock of the big flat stone, so that if we speak of 'The Rock of Carrickleck' we are guilty of tautology as in the case of The Naul.

Eanach, a marsh, is very common in Louth; *Annagh*, pluralized sometimes Annaghs, and Annies. Annyheem, the little marsh, Rathanna, the rath of the marsh.

Mullach, a hill, gives the Mullagh and Mullacrew, Mullaghban etc.

These few basic words by no means exhaust the list of natural features that form the basis of place names, but I must pass to a few which derive from man-made things, and will begin the list with *Áth*, a ford or river crossing which preceded the 'Droichead' or bridge. We have them combined in Droichead Átha: the bridge of the ford. Ardee, Baile Átha Fhirdia, Athboy Áth Buí – boy is *buí*. *Ceis*, a wicker bridge as in bog drains etc., gives Kish in the anglicised form of place names. *Dún*, a (strong) structure, is also a common element: Dundalk, Dun Dealgan. Viking influence gives us dalk and Dunderry – but Dunleer is Lann Léire, house of penitence (c.f. *lann* in words like leabharlann).

Caiseal, a strong fortification: one might imagine it was a translation of the English Castle but the strong round stone forts to which this name was given existed in Ireland from very early times. The word is an example of the many words in Irish which came to us from Latin (in this case Castellum). Drumcashel in Co. Louth gives the correct pronunciation, but there is a tendency for people in modern times to say 'Castle' as being more 'refined.' Many other names of course are properly called Castle from a Norman or later Castle.

Rath was a structure which enclosed a dwellinghouse and seems to have differed very little from a lios – *Lios*, as in Lismullen, Lisrenny. Both these are common. Often the *th* sound of Rath is preserved in the Anglicised version giving us a clue about when the modern Irish pronunciation of Ráth became *Rá* as in Rathanna (Eana, a personal name probably); Rathmore, the big rath; Belrath (Bel from *béal*, a mouth), the entrance to a rath. This Bel (*béal*) is not always easy to distinguish from *baile*, a house, homestead or townland, so common that we need not dwell on it.

The coming of Christianity brought us a new set of place names, called from the churches Kill, Donagh, *Teampall*, Eglish, *Seipeal*, all to be found around us: Donaghmore, the great church, Donaghpatrick, Patrick's church, Kilbride, Kilmurry etc. Some of the Kills however mean woods from the Irish *Coill* and it needs a study of the locality to come on the meaning and often it is not possible.

Various kinds of trees come frequently into place names, the most common being the oak *Dair* or *Doir*, and oak wood *Dairí* (dim. *Doirín*) as in Dunderry, Derrymore, Derrypatrick, Dorrinidaly, but we have also the ash, in the townland of *Fuinnseog* in Louth ang. Ashville, Ardsallagh, the height of the Sallies, Ath Trum, Tramman etc. (of the elders), to name only a few.

Two common words that sound rather alike to the non Irish speaker are *riasg* for moory land and *riabhach* for the colour grey or brownish and mottled. The former gives us Rooskey and Balriask, both near us here, and the latter Cloughrea, the grey stone, Reaghstown in Louth, and others. Collon, like Sliabh gCuillean, maybe from Holly or possibly hazel (*coll*).

Time does not permit me to give any more of these basic words, though it is a pity not to deal with such common ones as *Cúl*, back (Coolammey); *Escar*, a sand hill (Rathesker); *Tulach*, a hill (Tully-); *Bothar*, road (Bohernambo, Batterstown, Bóriach); *Tobar*, a well.

I must however refer to one or two later developments: first the Danish invasions in the 8th to 10th century. Invaders in all countries take native words as they find them: witness the Indian words in North America (e.g. Alabama). The chief noticeable word the Danes left us is *sta* which was their word for *teach* or *tig*, a house. The words were sufficiently alike anyhow so that an Irishman would recognise Tigh or Teach Cullan, Cullin's house, as Sta Cullan, and so we have Stackallen. There is a church in Kilbeg parish called Staholmog, from a saint, but the local pronunciation is still Histyholmog. Also Danish is the element *ey*, an island as in Ireland's Eye and Lambay.

In Norman and English times – and in general during recent centuries – any new names were in the main family names linked with part of an existing place name like Castleblaney which was formerly a MacMahon Castle, Jordanstown, Castleplunkett, Drakestown.

There were many translations some of them quite literal and correct like Kingscourt from Dún an Rí, but there were several very strange and ludicrous ones, e.g. Mooretown at Ardcath was Baile an Churraig 'the town of the moor or marsh', Phoenixtown (Martry) is 'the town of the *Fionnoig*' (scald crows) – c.f. Phoenix Park. Sometimes only the *baile* was translated as in Carnstown. The Mollies in Navan (*mallaí*, brows); Mount Sion for Cnoc Sidheán (fairy dwelling).

There are hidden delights when travelling round the county and reflecting on almost three thousand years of marking the landscape by our Gaelic forebears. We find a faint echo of the *Partraigi*, an earlier people who 'were settled between Crossakiel and Kells' as Paul Walsh tells us, and whose naming of the range, the Partry Mountains, in Co. Mayo is a rare survival of the millennia. Our place names, as we have seen, chronicle more recent arrivals, Vikings, Normans, and English. We hope that your study of place names and appreciation of this long history will inform whatever changes in habitation are in store for us.

Sources:
Ordnance survey Letters by John O Donovan and Eugene O Curry 1839.
History of Dioceses of Meath by Dean Cogan published in two volumes in 1862 and 1867.
Irish Place Names, P.W. Joyce (1877-1915). This contains a vocabulary of the root words from which Irish place names are most generally formed, with a considerable selection of those names.
Leinster States and kings in Christian times, Paul Walsh (see Nollaig Ó Muraíle *Irish Leaders and Learning through the Ages).*

John O Donovan was a nineteenth-century Irish scholar who worked in the Irish Ordnance Survey from 1830 until 1842 apart from a brief period in 1833. Eugene O Curry also worked on the Ordnance survey from 1835 to 1842. In 1854 he was appointed Professor of Archaeology and Irish History in the newly-founded Catholic university. In the following year he commenced the first of the two series of public lectures which later led to his most important works, *Manuscript Materials of Irish History* and *The Manners and Customs of the Ancient Irish.*

History of Kildalkey

Notes for a talk to the Irish Countrywomen's
Association, 1967.

Kildalkey from the time of St Patrick was a place of importance as a church, and afterwards as a monastery for 500 or 600 years, and even since then it has had an honourable if not so spectacular a place in history.

The name suggests that a church was founded by someone called Dealg or Deilge, but we do not know anything more about the founder – if such he was. We do know that there was a saint called St Trena of Cill Dealgan whom some historians say was a close friend of St Patrick; that he was a Bishop sent from Rome and had a church at Creelbach on the banks of the Brosna where he entertained St Patrick before he came to this place. Dealgan may have been the owner of the site, and it may have been Rath Dealgan. It is certain that then, as now, churches were built at important places – often a converted chief gave his rath and went to live elsewhere. Often old graveyards are circular and seen to be on raths. Other evidence of importance is the number of raths and rath names – Magh Ratha, Rath Chianain, Rath Chormaic etc. Perhaps the things that last longest are earthworks and names. You may imagine each of these with an important house of wood with rings around it; chiefs hunting and having their meetings and feasts, and perhaps some sort of celebrations at the well or on the banks of the Torrai.

Magh Ratha above all suggests that it commanded the whole plain, and the fact that from the first we get historic certainty that it was a place of residence – it was given in early Norman times to Nugent – shows the kind of continuity well authenticated elsewhere. Perhaps the chief lived where Moyrath Castle now stands and that the first church was here nearby in the old graveyard.

When monasteries began to be founded there was one here. In the martyrology of Tallaght there is St Ciarnain and St Dillan, feast of both on 31st January, both said to be of Cill Dealga. Are they the same person? Early abbots? It was a monastery of importance, for in the Annals there is reference to the deaths of various abbots from about 700 onwards, for nearly 200 years. Some are described as scribes which suppose a scriptorium, and one is even a Bishop. Its extent? One who knows the fields around might be able to trace the shape of wall foundations (and aerial photographs?) The name Cluan Mór is suggestive – but there are many other Cluans such as Cloneylogan.

Where does Dymphna fit into all this? In monastic 'cities' it was usual to have a convent in proximity to a monastery. Picture Clonmacnoise, Kildare or Kells – the various arts and crafts, leather, parchment, inks, quills – the food, grain, milk, clothes, vestments – the sacred vessels and the work of nuns in such a community. Dympna may well have been the foundress of this convent.

The legend is that she was daughter of king of Oirgealla, reared by a Christian foster mother who had her baptised by St Generbran. Her father – still pagan? – planned marriage for her, but she wished to be nun and fled to Kildalkey. The father pursued her there, and she fled with Genebran and two attendants to Antwerp in Belgium, gave silver coin to the innkeeper, and then found refuge in a wood nearby (and was perhaps joined by others). Father followed her, and gave the same kind of coin at the same inn, and the innkeeper told him of the previous travellers. He and his men followed and slew Generbran, and when Domhnait refused to return, the king ordered his men to kill her. When they refused, he killed her himself. It is said that at her death a well sprung up. The local people buried her and venerated her as a saint. In time, a church was built and her relics were transferred there (her feast is May 15th). In the town of Gheel she is remembered, and is said to cure disease of the mind. It may well be that a legend of another woman saint has been incorporated into Damhnait's story in folk tradition. Whatever the truth, the holy well at Kildalkey has borne her name through the centuries, and as this could not happen without cause it is safe to think that it is on or near the site of her convent.

When the Danish invasions began about 800, there was an end to the Golden Age of Kildalkey – to manuscripts, gold work and all the rest. In 885 it was burned by the Danes, and unlike some other places it does not seem to have recovered its former greatness, though it must have continued to be important enough. In about 1050 when the Danes had been defeated and the Church was being reorganised, it was given to Kells. The Charter in Book of Kells gives the grant of Kildalkey with its territory and land to "God and Colmcille for ever" by Conor O Maolsheaclann King of Meath.

When the Normans came, a Nugent got Maynooth and the parish seems to have been important – in 1402 Rev. Robert Montain, Pastor, became Bishop of Meath, and there are many other references. In 1418 Edmund Earl of March and Ulster owned the manor of Kildalkey and gave its church of St Mary's to St Mary's Abbey, Trim. At the Reformation (1542) St Mary's Trim and its possessions went to Sir Anthony St Leger, but in 1617 James I gave St Mary's Trim and Kildalkey to Sir Thomas Ashe of Trim.

It is likely that the church was extensively rebuilt by early Normans but that the monastic buildings, wherever they were, fell into ruin, and possibly the stones were used in Nugent castle and other buildings. Churches often continued to be used for Catholic worships for some time, when the local lord (as Nugent) did not conform. It was more a case of property than dogma for a long time. Even when Elizabeth tried to make the Reformation a reality, there was a scarcity of clergy: livings were held by Englishmen who never saw the places and employed a renegade Irish 'Minister' to serve, often of lower class.

By 1612 (70 years after Henry's confiscation), a report says the church was ruinous but the chancel was repaired. Seventy years later, Dopping (Protestant Bishop) in 1682 reports a Papist priest named Thomas Nugent in the parish. However, he would not have officiated in the church which was in Protestant hands, and probably little used. When James II came to throne of England in 1685 the Catholic gentry in many places began making repairs (the wells at Tullaghanoge and Iskeroon, for example, were repaired by the Barnwalls) and there may have been some repairs done here by Nugents or Nangles – we don't know – but on May 9th 1691 this Father Nugent (note that the clergy belonged to old Norman families) was appointed Pastor of Kildalkey, i.e. he would have celebrated Mass in the church. A few weeks later the Battle of the Boyne ended the short Catholic supremacy.

Fr Nugent must have died within the next few years, for in 1702 there is a letter from a Fr Geoghegan to Mrs Nangle of Kill (Kildare) whose chaplain he had been, saying that Mass was being celebrated in the open air and asking help to build a little chapel. We do not know if he got it. Dr Tyrrell died in 1692. Fr Geoghegan died shortly after, for a letter in May 1703 from George Nangle to Dr Michael Plunkett V.G. claims the right of nominating a successor.

The Penal Laws were at their worst during these years of Queen Anne (and it was the period of Swift) but the religious orders were holding on in secret – the Dominicans of Trim at Dunore and the Franciscan at Courtown, and they ministered in parishes as well (Fr Weybourne O.F.M. was P.P. of Kildalkey; he died about 1719 and is buried in Clonmacduff).

Bad as times were it is strange to see the squabbles between seculars and regulars, and between Bishops and lay patrons. There is a letter from parishioners to Dr MacEgan dated 1748 asking to have someone appointed during litigation with Nangle in Kildalkey who wanted a Franciscan, while the Bishop wanted secular priest. Arbitration by the Bishop of Kilmore and Lord Trimblestown (in 1749) decided in favour of his [Trimblestown's] cousin Nangle. Since the letter refers to Nangle taking vestments from the chapel by force, it appears there was some sort of building there – not of course the old one which was in Protestant hands, but probably a very humble one. Where was it? The present school site?

The Penal Laws were less stringent as the century went on and a Fr O Reilly (1782-94) repaired and partly rebuilt the chapel and erected a belfry, which was against the law; and on a complaint from the Rector of Athboy he had to remove it. It is said that the bell was hung in the branches of a tree for years. Fr Richard (1814-30) built a chapel and two schools (his epitaph is in Athboy, but the slab here says of the church that it was 'restaurata 1815').

As regards schools, Dr Plunkett (appointed 1779) noted one school in 1788, but later, in the Education report for 1826, there were two (Fr Richard's schools?). The Report says it was established in 1824 in the townland of Cloneylogan, built of mudwall by the parish and furnished at total cost of £150. Lewis (1837) says Darnley gave an acre of land and £20; J. Stack-Murphy gave £20 and also £30 for a school in Carnile. Fr O'Connell (1830-7), writing to ask to get under the National Board (1831 onwards) says there were five wretched schools in the parish and that the children must derive "the most worthless education." He proposed to build a school in Carnile. He adds that these other schools would cease "if the teachers in Kildalkey school were enabled to teach the children free." It must be noted that this condemnation of the hedge schools may have been made to strengthen the case for getting under the National Board, as Kildalkey did in 1834 and Carnile in 1843.

By this time the Nangles seem to have stopped living in Kildalkey. In 1812 a James Nangle died there – he was, it is said, born in Spain and elegantly educated and was an important and dignified member of the Catholic councils for Emancipation. It appears that after his death there was no Nangle left and the place passed to a Hodgins (perhaps a nephew) who lived in Dublin, but nevertheless took an interest in the parish, for when he died in 1831 he left £1000 for the erection of almshouses and £60 a year for the inmates who had to be natives of the parish. It was just at this time that Fr O Connell was agitating to get his schools recognised, and it seems that Mr Hodgins left nothing for school building.

So on the eve of the Famine Kildalkey had its chapel, bell and all, two national schools and in spite of all Fr O Connell had said, there were still hedge schools. The people had great respect for the old masters, many of them men of great learning. Fr Meagher says that years later a Mr Scott was teaching Latin and Maths and boys left the National school at 12 or so to go to him for higher study. He probably had night school also.

Who was first national teacher? The priest was by this time living in the present parochial house, as tenant of the Hodgins. Previously priests had lived in a house near the graveyard. Where was it? And what of the old church? It had remained neglected through the centuries and when Dean Cogan saw it in about 1860, there remained the choir arch, 8'4" x 6'1" at base; a square belfry tower at the west, high and ivy covered, and a considerable portion of the walls – he says it "presented a sense of melancholy desolation."

By that time Kildalkey had had its share of the horrors of famine and clearances, but the people did not take it all lying down. Back in '98 they and the boys of Bohermeen were the only ones in South Meath to have gone to join the Wexford men. The October before the Rising, Dr Plunkett at confirmation preached: "the taking of arms by night last summer from the respectable inhabitants of the parish reprobated." When he came the next October he does not note what he preached about, though the previous day (Sunday 14th) he spoke in Trim on "the folly and guilt of the late rebellion, a violation of Catholic principles, a departure from the ancient and modern practice of real Christians." Next time (July 1799) he only spoke of cursing, swearing, thieving, stealing and neglect of Sacraments, and afterwards he dined and spent the night at Clowne (in Dowdall's probably). (The Nugents seem to have been dispossessed in Cromwell's time.)

In Fenian times Kildalkey was again active. Among others there was a young man named Patrick MacNamee, then aged 26, who was a member of the Leinster Directory. He had gone to Scott's academy at the age of 12 and was said to be a scholar, linguist and historian. He is still remembered, I am sure, as the poet of Kildalkey, and perhaps some of you can recite some of his poems not to be found anywhere in print. We know very little about the activities of the Fenians, except that two guns found in Tuite's thatch (Clonmore) a few years ago show that the boys had again raided for arms. In this Fenian year, you would be doing a gracious service to the men who rose in dark and evil days, if you would collect and write down all the traditions that survive – and there are more than you might imagine. In doing this you would not be going so far from your primary intention of restoring the Holy well, for it seems that MacNamee, poet and Fenian, sometime before the end of his life (c1900?) collected money and did some repairs on the church. Some local people must surely remember this, and in inaugurating your effort to further preserve Tobar Domhnatan and the whole of the ancient site you will be also paying a not inappropriate tribute to the men who marched to Tallaght a hundred years ago – for they realised as did all patriots that a country with no care for its history is a country already dead. Kildalkey – Cill Dealgan Domhnatan - will, please God, not allow our Irish tradition to die in this generation.

Lewis, Samuel: *A Topographical Dictionary of Ireland, with Historical & Statistical Descriptions,* London 1837.
Ni Chonmhidhe Piskorska, Meadhbh: *Holy Wells dedicated to Women Saints: Brid, Gobnait and Damhnait,* unpublished essay for Diploma in Irish Folklore, N.U.I. Dublin 1995 (a copy is deposited with Meath County Library).

St Dympna's Well was reopened and blessed as part of a local project in 2000.

TLACHTGHA

A lecture read at an outing to Tlachtgha under the
auspices of Meath Archaeological and Historical
Society, 11 August 1957.

Other lectures concerned with historic sites such as
Trim, Tara, and Stella's Cottage are also among
Margaret Conway's manuscripts.

Seventy-three years ago, in the month of August 1884, the Society of Antiquarians were invited to meet here on this hill where we are assembled today. A paper was prepared for the occasion by a young man from the district, a clerical student in Maynooth – the twenty-one year old Eugene O Growney. I had that paper before me as I prepared this lecture and I could not but marvel at the amount of research this boy had done to produce a record, very condensed indeed, of the many events connected with this site from the dawn of history to that awful scene of slaughter in Cromwell's camp in 1649, after which date the silence of death and the peace of despair fell upon Tlachtgha.

It is always difficult to know where to begin in dealing with a place whose associations are partly historic and partly prehistoric. I have decided for the sake of clarity that we start at the first century of the Christian era, in the time of Tuathal Teachtmhar, who founded the Kingdom of Meath with its four Royal Residences: Teamhair, Uisneach, Tlachtgha and Tailte. If you keep this in mind, and locate from where we stand the other three hills, we can, before the end of this lecture, work back to what is to the historian partly legend and partly conjecture in the long ages before. Teamhair (Tara) lies about twelve miles east by south of us, Uisneach over 30 miles south west, and Tailte some 8 miles to the north east.

From legendary times there were five provinces in Ireland (from whence the Irish word for province *Cúige,* a fifth). These were at an early period Uladh (Ulster), Laighean (Leinster), Connacht and Mumha (Munster) which consisted of two provinces – North and South Munster. These divisions were not static and in any case were little more than a memory in the third century B.C. when reliable history begins. By then the most powerful centres were Uladh in the north east and Laighean in the south east. The famous Conchubhar Mac Neasa at about the beginning of the Christian era ruled the Ulster province from Eamhan Macha (near Armagh) with the aid of an army of warriors known as the Craobh Ruadh (Red Branch).

Leinster was ruled by the powerful Eochaidh Feidleach, who put his daughter Medhbh (Maeve) on the throne of Connacht. Under her rule the rivalry with Ulster resulted in the seven years' war known in Irish heroic literature as the Táin Bo Cuailgne (The Cattle-raid of Cooley). The result was the decline of Ulster as the greatest power in the country. It appears from the sagas that contingents from all parts of Ireland were on Maeve's side, and that as a result of the war there developed a new and more organised kingdom with its centre in the central plain. This power was to dominate all Ireland, though there were centuries of opposition from the older people of Uladh and Laighean.

This central dynasty seems to have become firmly established about a century after the wars of the Táin, and its first great monarch was Tuathal Teachtmhar (the Lawful). It is said that he decided to create a new Kingdom to be the mensal land of the Ard-Ri (High King) by cutting off a part of each of the four provinces that bounded one another in the Central Plain. The Five Fifths was not then in existence but the memory of it may have influenced Tuathal's decision. The new kingdom was called Midhe (Meath), said by most philologists to mean "Middle" from a Celtic root allied to the Latin 'medium'. Some derive it from the word for a plain (in modern Irish Maighe-anglicised Moy). Tara, the new Royal Residence, was in the Leinster part, Tailte in the Ulster part, Uisneach in the Connacht part, and our hill, Tlachtgha, in the Munster part. (It may be noted that these four hills were already sacred places and this aspect will be discussed later.) It would appear that Tuathal had a Royal Residence on each of these hills, and that he paid them state visits in turn. From descriptions in early Irish poetry, the palaces of Pre-Christian Ireland were of great magnificence. There are references to lime-white walls, pavilions thatched with brilliant coloured feathers, pillars inlaid with bronze and gold and hangings of costly embroidery. The ladies of the royal household had a special house on the sunny side of the hill – it was called the Grianán (sunny place). Wood, so plentiful in those days in the plain, was the usual building material; therefore when the palaces were abandoned (in the fifth and sixth century) they soon fell into decay, and the only remains today are the ridges of clay which marked the sites of foundations, and the concentric rings of clay which carried defensive palisades. No excavations have been made at Tlachtgha, but from the work done on Tara during the past decade we can assume with fair certainty that the spade would yield up on Tlachtgha the traces of extensive habitations.

Abandoned or not, Tlachtgha was a landmark and gathering place right up to the days of the last independent High King – Ruaidhri O'Connor – who held a meeting there in the year 1167. Time will not permit a detailed account of all the references to Tlachtgha in the annals and in oral tradition: a few will have to suffice.

The first is the tradition that St Patrick visited this hill. There are the remains of an ancient church in the vicinity called Teampall Cuimhne (translated as the church of Remembrance). The local tradition is that at this spot St Patrick remembered where he had left his Mass Books on the course of his journey. That is the sort of fantastic explanation that local scholars invent for a name they do not understand, but from what we know of St Patrick's journeys from hill to hill – Slane, Tara, Tailte etc. – we may be certain that he visited here.

The next record is better authenticated. After the Danes had been defeated at Clontarf by Brian Boru in 1014, many of them remained in the coast towns which they had founded. Dublin was their greatest stronghold on the east coast, and from there they made a raid into Meath in 1022. They were defeated by the High King, Maol Seachnaill (Malachy) at Ath Buidhe Tlachtgha – the Yellow Ford of Tlachtgha. As you can see, a river flows below us, and there was a ford or crossing place where the modern town of Ath Buidhe (Athboy) now stands. It is a common development everywhere: people settled near the ford, which in course of time was replaced by a bridge. (Compare 'Drogheda' – Droichead Atha – the Bridge of the Ford.)

The century following the defeat of the Danes was a turbulent one: a series of wars following the breakdown of an older order. The High Kings from the time of Tuathal had been drawn from the same ruling family, but in Danish times Brian of Munster had broken the tradition by usurping the High Kingship. After his death at Clontarf, Malachy, of the old dynasty, resumed office and, as has been said, defeated the Danes of Dublin here in 1022. But after his death there were periodic contentions for the High kingship between various great families. During one of these wars Athboy was burned by the O Briens (descendants of Brian). Eventually order was restored under the O Connors of Connacht, a branch of the old ruling family, and the country settled down to what appeared to be a new era of peace and progress. Ruaidhri O Connor called in 1167 a great council of the principal clergy and laity of the country and they met at Ath Buidhe Tlachtgha to discuss the reorganisation of church and state. When you hear the names of even a few of the people who attended, you will realise that Athboy must have been a considerable place if it could provide them with food and shelter. No doubt pavilions were erected for them, and the meeting itself probably took place in a large and elegant structure on top of the hill itself. There were the Archbishops of Armagh and Tuam and Dublin (the last was later to be known to history as St Laurence O Toole). With these were the chief abbots and a huge concourse of attendant clergy. All the chiefs of Meath, Ulster, Breffini, Oriel and Kildare were there, with 13,000 horsemen.

At this conference all sorts of matters were settled amicably, including the exact boundaries of the territories of the various chiefs. Two years later Tighernan O Ruairc, Chief of Breffini, was confirmed as ruler of this district of Tlachtgha, on the border land of Meath. Everyone was happy about the future, but alas, in a very short time, Dervorgilla, wife of Ruairc, was instrumental in bringing in new invaders – the Normans – and so setting at naught the plans so happily inaugurated at the great conference of Ath Buidhe Tlachtgha.

Hugh de Lacy was given the Kingdom of Meath by King Henry II of England, but O Ruairc did not submit easily to having his territory included. A conference was arranged between himself and de Lacy here on the hill. Each left his bodyguard at a distance and they met alone and unarmed with only an interpreter – one Domhnall O Ruairc. (Incidentally the fact that an O Ruairc could speak Norman-French would point to intercourse across the Irish sea before the invasion.) The Four Masters record that during the conference the captain of de Lacy's bodyguard crept up and treacherously murdered O Ruairc. The contemporary Norman account says that the captain (Griffith by name) had a dream the night before in which he saw his master being attacked by the Irish chief, and to forestall such a calamity, he got his blow in first! O Ruairc's head was severed and spiked on the fortress of Dublin (the fort which preceded the present Dublin Castle). His body was gibbeted, feet upward, at the northern gate of the city.

Gradually as the Normans made themselves masters of the Central Plain, and when the Pale, or Boundary Fence, was built to defend the settlement, it passed more or less along the river through Athboy, till on the Trim side it crossed the river to take in the Castle of Trimblestown and the town of Trim itself, the capital of Anglo Norman Meath. Parts of the pale can still be detected in wide fences here and there on the Dublin side of the river. Athboy itself was a strong walled frontier town, with defensive walls and castles; even its monasteries were more like fortresses than religious houses, and their occupants were Norman monks of the new religious orders that the invaders had brought with them. The town was often attacked, and sometimes sacked, by the Irish of the O Ruairc country – the Reillys, Farrellys etc. The town had its typical Market Cross, said to have been buried in the middle of the present main street during the Cromwellian wars. In times of peace however there was much trade in wines and other continental luxuries which the native Irish imported through Galway. The wines were stored in vaults still existing under the houses in the main street, and we may guess that the revenue benefited very little from them. Remains of the town wall exist at the junction of the Kildalkey road, and behind the present Catholic Church. Connacht Street preserves the memory of the Connacht Gate. The Protestant church is pre-Reformation; the tower is 14th century.

We hear little of the hill itself during these centuries – the town is known in the Irish records as Ath Buidhe and in English ones as Athboy. By the year 1640 the descendants of the first Norman planters were menaced themselves by the laws of England, which they still regarded as their mother country. Most of these Lords of the Pale had adhered to the Catholic Faith, and now threatened with Penal legislation and with the confiscation of their lands, they made reluctant alliance with the native Irish chiefs, whose leader was Eoghan Rua O Neill. This scion of the great northern royal house had won fame as one of the finest soldiers in Europe where he served in the army of the king of Spain. He was the obvious selection as commander-in-chief in the war which was now beginning, but traditional jealousy caused the Palesmen to restrict his command to the Ulster forces. In the course of the war however the Leinster army was unable to hold its ground against the English forces. Eoghan Rua came down to their assistance, and having taken the town of Athboy, set up his camp on the Hill of Tlachtgha. He made entrenchments on the remains of the original ring fort, and these ridges at present rather complicate the study of the site by archaeologists.

A few years later Eoghan Rua was dead, the Confederate Army was not able to stand up to meet the new forces under Cromwell, and after the massacre of Drogheda there was little further attempt at defence in Leinster. Cromwell marching south is said to have camped on the hill, on the site of O Neill's entrenchments. The ruling (Norman) family of the district were the Plunketts of Rathmore. There today stand the ruins of their Castle and their beautiful church. Cromwell summoned Plunkett, Lord Rathmore, to a conference, and Plunkett rode to the hill accompanied by his seven sons. Tradition says that their mother begged them not to go as she had dreamed that they would all be slaughtered. Whether she dreamed or not, the whole Plunkett family was wiped out that day. (There is a legend that the youngest boy escaped, but there is no reliable record of his name in later history.) The Cromwellian cannon was directed on the Castle of Rathmore, leaving it in ruins.

It is historic fact that most of the land of Ireland was confiscated in Cromwellian times and given to soldiers and 'undertakers' but the circumstances of the confiscation in this district is a living legend to this day. There was a man named Bligh in Cromwell's army, described as a butcher, but more probably the man in charge of providing food for the army on the march. Cromwell was grateful to him for the efficient manner in which he had discharged this duty, so when the Plunketts were disposed of, he gave Bligh all the land he could see from the hill, looking south. The first high ground in that direction was the Hill of Kilmer (parish of Ballivor) some ten miles away. Up to the early days of this century when most of the property was sold to the Irish Land Commission, the Bligh Estate extended to this hill. A later Bligh was ennobled as Lord Darnley, and a descendant of his a hundred years ago was the friend and neighbour of Charles Dickens when the novelist lived at Gad's Hill. The Darnley house was Cobden Hall, and there the Lords lived for most of the time, only coming to Ireland for the hunting and shooting. Their home here, Clifton Lodge, is still occupied, though the Darnleys have passed out of Irish history.

I have said that the name Tlachtgha dropped out of common speech, and with the gradual loss of the language it was forgotten altogether, and the name Hill of Ward was substituted. The origin of this name is doubtful: some say it is from 'Bard' (Cnoc an Bhaird, the Hill of the Bard); others that Ward is a personal name, and others that the hill was a lookout or place of ward (guard). The great antiquarians of the 19th century had doubts about the location of the ancient Tlachtgha. John O Donovan when working on the Ordnance Survey took great trouble in establishing the identity of the place. He was hampered in his work by the difficulty in consulting manuscripts housed in Dublin and comparing the information they recorded with what he learned on the spot. So he was in the habit of writing to his colleagues in Dublin asking them to look up sources for him, and fortunately his letters are preserved, so that his difficulties are our gain. There is in Meath County Library a copy of the letters relating to the county, as prepared by the late Rev. Michael O Flanagan. Here is the letter relating to Tlachtgha:

Authrumiae, Augi, 8, 1836

Dear Sir,
Yesterday (Sunday) I travelled about sixteen miles in search of traditions about Tlachtgha, but was very much disappointed, as very few of the aboriginal methians are now in the neighbourhood.

I visited the hill (accompanied by an old soldier who was as anxious as myself to discover the site of Tlachtgha) and was puzzled for a long time about the shape of the fort, until at last we observed that the original palace of Tuathal had been variously dissected and modelled into a modern entrenchment. The original fort consisted of four (perhaps five) concentric rings, with a moat in the centre now much lowered. The diameter of the outer circle (as well as I could ascertain from the irregularity of the ground) is 136 yards. From what remains of this fort which I now assume to be Tlachtgha, it will appear that several of the rings of Telton have been levelled; the circle remaining there at present seems to have been one of the external ones. The internal circles have been so much broken up to form the fossae, valla and redoubts of a modern *foslongphort*, that no peculiar features can now be observed as belonging to the original fort, except deep hollows, and one (i.e. one not well acquainted with the mode of entrenchment in 1641) should not too hastily assume that these were not formed during the Rebellion of 1641.

This hill, the highest in the neighbourhood, stands over the town of Athboy (Ath Buidhe Tlachtgha), three-quarters of a mile to the north-east, but as you look down the summit of the hill, Athbuidhe Tlachtgha looks quite close to you in the hollow beneath, and like Taillteann, commands an extensive view of the country round.

After carefully viewing this fort, which now stands in the middle of a field of oats, and after listening to a long lesson from my military guide upon the nature of entrenchments, redoubts and other things of which, no doubt, I knew very little, I set out in search of the chief antiquarian of the district, a Mr Eaglison (Mac an Iollair) who lives on the margin of the bog of Rathmore. I found him by chance at home and questioned him very cautiously about the Hill of Ward. He said that tradition handed down very little about it except that it was a place of meeting established for Bards regarded by Tuathal Teachtmar, that the fort was formed into an entrenchment by Owen Roe O Neill during the War of 1641, and afterwards by Cromwell.

I would like to direct your attention to the suggestion that there were none of the natives left, and this thirteen years before the famine and the beginning of the great clearances; also to the fact that the old soldier was probably a veteran of the British army of Napoleonic times, for after the French Revolution Irish soldiers no longer went to the Brigades of France. Mr Eagliston seems to have been knowledgeable for later in the letter it is stated that he told O Donovan much about Ros na Riogh and other sites far distant from Rathmore. In other letters O Donovan mentions getting place names from Irish speakers and from English speakers.

The impression we get is that the district was altogether bilingual, some preferring to use one language, some the other. O Growney's written accounts show how rapid was the deterioration during the next thirty-five years – the result of a generation of 'National Education.'

Now having brought the story of Tlachtgha from the dawn of definite history down to almost our own times, I would like to go back for a few moments to the period before the founding of the Kingdom of Meath. For Tlachtgha was old in fame when Tuathal chose it as the site of a palace – how old we cannot say in years, or even centuries. The annals say that Tuathal celebrated the festival of Samhain at Tlachtgha, thus continuing the ancient custom. Samhain is the beginning of winter; and the word, used in modern Irish for the month of November ('Samhfhuin .i. bás an tsamraid'). We know the feast of Samhain today as Hallow Eve, but there is nothing hallowed, in the Christian sense, about the games and customs associated with it: the nuts and apples, the claw of wool in the limekiln, the rings, the divination by ivy leaves and melted lead are obviously remains of pagan practices – rites of thanks giving for the harvest gathered, and of commemoration of the death which winter symbolises.

Before the coming of the Celts (or Milesians) some three centuries before Christ, the two great feasts of the year were Bealtaine and Samhain. Bealtaine, celebrated by the lighting of fires, heralded the coming of Summer, and Tuathal re-established this feast on the Hill of Uisneach. There was also an Autumn Festival, consisting chiefly of Athletic contests, which was celebrated at Tailteann. It was called Lugh-neasa and has given the modern Irish Lughnasa (August). There is less record of the spring festival, which has been replaced in Christian times by St Brigid's Day.

Perhaps we may suppose that it was celebrated in a special way on the fourth hill – Tara. It appears from place names and other evidence that the great feasts were celebrated elsewhere through the country, always on hilltops, but possibly, in every kingdom, a particular hill began the celebration. I say this because we know that though Samhain was inaugurated here at Tlachtgha, there was, some time later, a great triennial assembly at Tara (Feis Teamhrach) where laws were reviewed and disputes settled. It lasted for three days before and three days after Samhain.

There is an earlier legend about this hill which gives it a special significance, and for a short account of it I am indebted to the little booklet *Royal Meath* by Rev. Donncadh O Meachair – both book and author are known to many of you. The legend says that the hill owes its name to a woman named Tlachtgha, back in the early days of the Tuatha Dé Danann (the Bronze Age people, probably 1800 – 300 B.C.). She it was who made the Roth Ramhach, or Rowing Wheel, the Lia or Flagstone, and the Coirthi or Pillarstone, three things of awful magical power, and she brought these three things with her from the east till she reached this hill, and there she remained and bore three sons, and there she died, and was buried in this Dún. Tailteann is named after Queen Taillte; Sliabh na Callaighe near Oldcastle is the Mountain of the Old Woman; Tara itself is said to be named after a woman – Tea. These legends, taken together, seem to suggest a connection from the very earliest times between the four hills. We now know that the hills at Loughcrew (Sliabh na Callaighe) contain numerous cairns of Bronze Age times, and recent excavations have shown that when Tara was chosen as a Royal Residence it was already a pagan cemetery of great antiquity. Indeed it was probably for their ancient sacred association that all the hill-sites were chosen as palaces. Therefore I think we would be justified in believing that we are standing today on top of a great burial mound, 'half as old as time.' Only excavation can tell the tale, and in that respect Tlachtgha has been sadly overlooked. Besides the visit of the Antiquarians in 1884, I can find no record of any pilgrimage to the spot. Even that event is not mentioned in the official records of the Royal [Dublin] Society. Fr O Growney's note is the only evidence that a visit was at least projected. We may therefore be the first organised group of people to come here, not for purposes of war or murder, but to pay homage to the ancient glory of Tlachtgha, where for four thousand years the ancient Dé Danann kings and queens lie buried, their ashes mingling with those of Gael and Dane, Norman and Cromwellian as they wait alike the Resurrection Morn.

Literature before and after Kinsale

A lecture, one in a course on Irish History and
Culture devised by Margaret Conway and given in
1967 by a group of scholars at *An Grianan*, the Irish
Countrywomen's Association centre, Termonfechin.
Other scholars included Helen Roe, one time
President of the Royal Society of Antiquaries,
Augustine Martin, lecturer in Anglo–Irish Literature
at the National University, Dublin and Proinsias O
Ceallaigh, senior inspector of Music at the
Department of Education.

We are accustomed to take the Battle of Kinsale, 1601, as the end of the Gaelic way of life in Ireland. Those of us who learned our history through the medium of English may not perhaps appreciate fully just what the Gaelic way of life meant; we perhaps think of the change as legal, the end of Brehon laws – something that could happen in a matter of months, or at most of a very few years, and we may not fully grasp the fact that you cannot legislate a civilisation out of existence. We may, too, underestimate the strength and dignity of the Gaelic civilisation, and think of it rather as of an extension of the sort of impoverished civil life that outsiders thought was in the Gaeltachtaí of half a century ago – 'illiterate' story tellers, 'ag seinn ceoil do phócaí folmha' – not as the patrician life, the aristocratic structure that it certainly was.

Therefore let us first look at the case of Maghnas O Domhnaill, prince of Tir Conaill, who flourished some seventy years before Kinsale. In 1527 he built a strong castle at Clifford. He spent the next five years in assembling all known manuscripts and oral traditions of St Colm Cille and collated them into a Life completed in 1532. I shall have to refer to this work again in talking about Irish Classical prose. It may have been partly on the strength of this that he was elected prince of Tir Conaill two years later, in fact in the very year that Silken Thomas and his five uncles were beheaded in the tower. Just before that Henry VIII had himself proclaimed head of the Church by the Dublin Parliament, but all this which to us looking back marks the beginning of a new conquest did not evidently seem important to the Irish princes – their position and permanence must not have seemed in any great danger, for two years later we find Manus and Conn Prince of the O Neills as usual raiding the English Pale (then a very small strip of land on the east coast).

Even the Dissolution of the Monasteries does not seem to have had much effect at first outside the Pale, and when in 1541 Henry invited all the Irish chiefs to a Parliament in Dublin in order to have the title 'King of Ireland' conferred on him, it seemed merely a matter of words. He was already 'Lord of Ireland', a sort of deputy grantee of the Pope, and now that he had broken with the Pope he had no right to the 'Lordship.' MacCartys, O Briens, O Neills were there and many others, including MacWilliam-Burke, a Gaelicised Norman lord. (The 'carrot' was succession by primogeniture.)

The business of the Parliament was done completely through Irish since not one of the chiefs – Irish or Anglo Norman – had a word of English except Butler Earl of Ormond who acted as interpreter for the officials from London. Only the poet of the O Donnells (O Hussey?) saw into the future when he composed this biting poem condemning the chieftains:

> *Fúbún fúibh, a shluagh Gaoidheal,*
> *ní mhair aoineach agaibh,*
> *Goill ag comhrainn bhur gcríche*
> *re sluaigh sithe bhur samhail.*

(Shame on you, o men of the Gael, not one of you has life in him, the foreigners are sharing your lands among themselves, you are like a phantom host.)

The poem went on to say that none of the MacCarthys follows Gaelic ways, the O Briens have turned their backs on their patrimony, Connacht and Leinster nobles have submitted, and O Neill has foolishly exchanged his kingdom for the title of Earl of Ulster:

> *Ó Domhnail Atha Seanaigh*
> *Nár ob deabhaidh ná doghraing,*
> *D'Éirinn fa mór an t-amhghar,*
> *do mheath Magnas Ó Domhnaill.*

Fúbún fán ngunna nGallghlas,
fúbún fán slabhra mbuidhe,
fúbún fán gcúirt gan Bhéarla
fúbún séanadh Mheic Mhuire.

(O Donnell of Ballyshannon who shirked not fight nor hardship, great is Ireland's dejection that Maghnas O'Donnell has failed her. Fúbún to the grey foreign gun, fúbún to the golden chain, fúbún to the court without English, fúbún to the denial of Mary's son.)

It is no wonder the chiefs did not see the writing on the wall for Irish culture. Two hundred years before, statutes had forbidden any of English extraction to speak or write in the Irish language and many similar acts had so little effect that when Queen Elizabeth, 30 years after this fúbún was written changed her language policy with a view to furthering the Reformation, she found scholars in the very heart of the Pale competent to translate the Bible into Irish (they spent 30 years at the job and the type, first ever, was later bought by Louvain). In 1578 the Chancellor said "all English with delight even in Dublin speak Irish." Forty years after Kinsale, Dr Dease Bishop of Meath was writing poems in Irish – in scholarly metres – to his friend Seámas Dubh Nuinnsionn (Nugent). They were both Anglo-Irish (there was no native Bishop in these Pale dioceses from the Norman Invasion till the Penal times) and he was by no means what we would describe as an Irish Patriot.

What was this Gaelic literature, that so attracted the Norman settlers? Let us look briefly at what led up to the sophisticated writing of professionals and amateurs in the 16th century. Pre-Christian learning in Ireland is believed to have been chiefly oral. When Latin learning came with St Patrick there may have been rivalry between the two traditions – the monasteries knew how to make vellum and their recording was in writing, but they seem to have learned to live together and, while the monasteries specialised in chronicling, the native schools produced the great prose sagas like the Táin, several of which a qualified *file* must be able to tell on demand. There were interspersed in them what we would call 'purple passages' in poetic language, if not in what we today would call verse. Much later, many of the greatest of these stories were written down, sometimes in summary, sometimes co-ordinated so that they were almost new works. But in the monastic schools themselves native learning was not abandoned for Latin, as happened in the whole Roman world where there was contempt for the 'barbarous' tongues of already conquered people. So quite early we have from the monasteries some of our most beautiful lyrics. The monasteries were above all the great chroniclers, and all our Annals, i.e. our early histories, derive from them.

The Viking raids from 800 on to nearly 1000 A.D. caused the destruction of innumerable manuscripts, and during the peaceful years of his reign Brian Boru did much to repair the damage. He sent scholars to the Continent to buy 'books' and study the latest in European scholarship. Scribes got to work at home in the schools copying all that was left and making new versions of the old oral tales as well as adaptations from Latin sources of Latin and Greek classics and religious material.

The monastic spirit, however, seemed to have weakened, here as in Europe, and in the 11th and 12th centuries there were great church reforms culminating in the introduction of the new religious orders – the Canons regular of St Augustine and St Bernard's great new order, the Cistercians, whose first Irish house was opened here in Mellifont in 1148. On their heels came the Norman invaders, and in much of the eastern part of the country and in pockets elsewhere they dominated the new monasteries so that the atmosphere was no longer conducive to the development of native learning. Here then the lay schools (Bardic schools) came into their own again – a phenomenon unknown I think elsewhere in Western Europe. Every chieftain had a school of which he was the patron and we hear of the scholar families – O Dalys, O Higgins, Coffeys, O Husseys (for by this time surnames were universal). Members of these families continued for centuries to adopt the profession of letters, and as they graduated some of them took service with other chiefs rather than their original patrons, so that we meet, for example, O Dalys in every part of Ireland. From 1200 A.D. at least the language, grammar, poetic metres and vocabulary appear to have been very highly developed, and the poems and other works, wherever in Ireland they may have been produced, are without a trace of dialect so that they could be appreciated, and were, by scholars here (and in Scotland up to the '45).

It is said that it took seven years training to make a qualified *file*. He was a great deal more than a rhymer: he was a gentleman of much substance, his advice was regarded as prophecy (the ancient *filí* were druids/seers) and a satire from him was as much to be dreaded as a decree of excommunication. (There are stories of satires which literally raised blisters on the victim.) But while poetry is what we chiefly associate with the term 'bardic schools' there was also a great deal of other learning – law, medicine, genealogy and the study of Greek and Latin classics.

It also appears almost certain that besides the special courses for professional men of learning, the schools also catered for the general literary education of the upper classes, for we find every evidence of amateur poets and men of letters all through the period. Every great house whether Irish or Norman had its *Duanaire*, a huge manuscript book into which were transcribed the praise poems, accounts of great deeds, and laments for the dead written for the family by the professional poets. Praise poems, genealogies etc. were first recited on great occasions, not by the *file* but by a bard with harp accompaniment. By the year 1300 the impetus of the Norman conquest had died down and the Norman lords had become largely Gaelicised. The new conquest did not begin till after the Wars of the Roses (1485).

You have all heard of the famous Gearoid Iarla, third Earl of Desmond – a Fitzgerald – who died in 1398. In the family *Duanaire*, the Book of Lismore, there are several of his poems in which there are references to what must have been the favourite stories of the time – Diarmuid and Gráinne, Naoise, Créidhe daughter of Guaire, etc.

In the early 1500s the library of the Earl of Kildare had 21 Latin, 11 French, 7 English and 20 Irish books, and a somewhat later Irish poet, Tadhg Dall O h-Uiginn (1591), has in his poems references not only to native tales but to Hercules, the wars of Troy, King Arthur – and also to lesser known French and Italian tales. This shows an enrichment of Irish literature from continental sources which was going on through all this century of dreadful war – the Desmond, Shane O Neill and O Neill /O Donnell wars. It would be wearisome to name all the adaptations and translations of the century. Besides, in the houses of princes and chiefs, Irish and Anglo Irish, there was still story telling at the end of a day, still the recitation of the great deeds of the chief and his ancestors, to the accompaniment of harp music – for all Irish poetry was meant to please the ear rather than the eye, and thus it suffers very much in translation. It also makes it very difficult to describe, and few of us can read classical Irish well enough to appreciate the originals.

The strict traditions of the schools tended to make the 'rules' of poetry too inflexible and the vocabulary contained words and phrases obsolete for centuries. But outside the 'bardic' poetry there were amateurs using simpler and more pleasing metres. The poets of the schools wrote for aristocrats and looked down on the lower orders, so that after the downfall of the Gaelic patrons one poet, typical of many, asks 'who will buy a poem.'

> *Ceist, cia do cheinneóchadh dán?*
> *a chiall is ceirteólas suadh,*
> *an ngéabha nó an ól le haon*
> *dán soar do bhéara go buan?*

Gé dán soin go snadhmadh bhfis,
gach margadh Ó chrois go crois
do shiubhail mé an Mhumhain leis –
ní breis é a-nuraidh ná a-nois.

Ceard mar so ní sochar dhán
gé dochar a dol fa lár,
uaisle dul ré déineamh coir,
gás briogh d'éinfhior dul re dán.

(Question! Who will buy a poem? Its meaning is genuine learning of scholars. Will anyone accept or does anyone wish for a noble poem which will make him immortal? Though this is a poem woven with knowledge, I have walked all Munster with it, every market from cross to cross, with nothing gained thereby from last year to this. Such art is profitless to me, though 'twere a pity it should decline; it were nobler to become a maker of combs – what use is it for anyone to take to poetry?)

The poets were very bitter about their loss of status, and some were too proud to adapt to new conditions. But when a couple of generations had passed with the prestige of the schools gone, the poets had to take to teaching or other occupations.

Immediately after Kinsale, men of vision could see the break up that was just beginning, and so perhaps instinctively began to collect chronicles and works of literature. During the first third of the 17th century we have the Annals of the Four Masters, a collection of all previous annals, written secretly in the Monastery of Donegal, and Keating's History of Ireland written secretly in the Glen of Aherlow. (Note: he was a Bishop and his name is not Irish.) No doubt the enlightened Protestants helped them, otherwise they could not have recourse to the earlier Mss which passed into lay hands at the Dissolution. Archbishop Ussher gave the Book of Kells to Trinity College and Dubhaltach Mac Foirbisigh went to live with Ware in Dublin to help him with his Antiquities [Sir James Ware, author

of The Antiquities and History of Ireland]. Louvain continued
with plenty of devotional works. All the prose of this period is
simple and direct – classical Irish casting off the academic fetters. A
contemporary of Keating was Captain Somhairle Mac Domhnall, a
soldier in the Spanish army of the Netherlands, one of those who left
Ireland after Kinsale. He got two scribes at Louvain to write for him
all the Finn ballads they could collect. These had evidently become
very popular outside the strict aristocratic circle. The romances
therein of which *Diarmuid and Gráinne* is best known became
regular themes for poets over the centuries. The *Dunaire Finn* is in
the Franciscan Library in Dublin.

Keating's history and his other works are examples of good Irish
prose, as was the Life of Colmcille by Magnus O Donnell already
referred to. They are simply and clearly written but without slang or
dialect as befitted works of devotion to be read by or to the common
people. As biographers they are not critical: the saints referred to are
credited with all the virtues; they work marvellous miracles, and if
a layman, even a king, insults them they immediately call down the
wrath of God on him. But they have a freshness and charm of the
age of faith.

There were of course many kinds of literature besides the praise
poems and the lives of saints – even Keating, bishop though he was,
has written a love poem, *A bhean lán de stuaim*, but in the century
of the penal laws, poetry which could be memorised was most likely
to survive. The poets used to meet now and then for a Court of
Poetry, particularly in Munster; gradually the 'court' became little
more than a few old men meeting in a tavern. But as the poetry
of the schools flickered out, Irish poetry, freed from the academic
tradition, blossomed into its own most beautiful verse, correct in
the simpler metrical forms. If O hIfearnáin found no one to buy
his poem on the eve of Kinsale, a century and a half later Séamus
Dall Mac Cuarta satirises the stinginess in *Tithe Chorra a Chait*
and Aodhagáin O Rathaille on his death bed rails at the loss of his

chief and his hope in a poem that begins *Cabhair ní ghoirfead go gcuirtear mé i gcrainn chomhrainn* (I will not ask for help till I am put in a narrow coffin), and ends with the magnificent and tragic declaration of *mórtas cine*, claiming his ancestors were poets to the MacCarthys for over a thousand years:

> *Stadfadsa feasta, is gar dom éag gan maill,*
> *Ó treascradh dreagain Leamhain, Léin is Laoi;*
> *Rachad-sa a haithle searc na Laoch don chill,*
> *Na flatha fá raibh mo shean roimh éag do Chríost.*

(I will cease now; death is nigh unto me without delay; Since the warriors of the Laune of the Lein and of the Lee have been laid low, I will follow the beloved among the heroes to the grave, those princes under whom were my ancestors before the death of Christ.)

Although composing most of their work in the popular song metre, Séamus Dall Mac Cuarta and Aodhagán O Rathille have both left us verse in 'dán díreach.' For if they hadn't been to school, they had met the scholars.

Oliver Goldsmith

A party of members of Meath Archaeological and
Historical Society paid a visit to the Lissoy and
Ballymahon district on 7 August 1939, at which this
lecture was delivered. The text was published in the
Westmeath Examiner.

Since its foundation two years ago, the Meath Archaeological and Historical Society have had a number of outings to places of antiquarian interest in the ancient Kingdom of Meath: Tara, the Lough Crew Hills, Slane, and other sites associated with the dawn or the early morning of history. To-day we are breaking new ground and catering for those members who in the words of a contemporary of Goldsmith, prefer 'the warm precincts of the cheerful day,' and sites and scenes nearer to us in time and in human interest. This is our excuse, if excuse were needed, for our visit to-day.

The loveliest village of the plain ….
Where smiling Spring her earliest visits paid,
And partying Summer's lingering blooms delayed.

We have called the Ballymahon-Athlone district 'the Goldsmith country' – the Tourist Association in their guide books refer to it more appropriately as 'the Poets' Country.' This is the district that in Goldsmith's youth rejoiced in the visits of that great blind poet and composer, Turlough O'Carolan, the Last of the Bards. He frequently visited at the house of Charles O'Connor, a friend of the Goldsmith family. Indeed he used to say 'When I am among the O'Connors the harp has the old sound in it,' and from him the young Goldsmith learned a passionate love of Irish music which he never lost. More than a century later John Keegan Casey was a familiar figure in this same district. Leo of 'leafy Tang' who saw by 'the singing river' Inny 'that dark mass of men' drilling by the Rising of the Moon. Some other items it may be our privilege to follow the footsteps of that gentle and great-hearted boy, but to-day we will go back in imagination to the Ireland of even darker days, the Ireland of Goldsmith's youth.

Let us imagine then that this is an August day, not in 1939, but in 1739, and that we have arrived by coach at the old inn at the crossroads, 'that house where nut-brown draughts inspired.' The good master welcomes us in and we observe:

The parlour splendours of that festive place:
The varnished clock that clicks behind the door;
The chest, contrived a double debt to pay,
A bed by night, a chest of drawers by day;
The pictures placed for ornament and use,
The Twelve Good Rules, the Royal Game of Goose;
The hearth, except when winter chilled the day,
With aspen bough and flowers and fennel gay,
While broken teacups, wisely kept for show,
Ranged o'er the chimney glistened in a row.

Perhaps among 'the gazing rustics ranged around' we may notice an odd-looking boy of eleven; he is hopping about on his short legs like a rather shy sparrow; his head is big, his face pitted with pock-marks; he is wearing the frayed pantaloons of decent poverty. There is little to distinguish him from the other urchins, for they are all chattering in their native Gaelic. If we were to ask who he was – though indeed it is most unlikely we should do so – we would be told that he was one of the Minister's sons, and that a decent man his father is surely, no way bigoted and very good to the poor, though indeed it is little he has for himself with eight children to support on a small living. So this is the little Oliver Goldsmith, and who, two hundred years ago, would have dreamed that lovers of English literature would one day journey over half the globe to see this very inn, and the home of his childhood and the church where his father preached, and all the other haunts he immortalised in *The Deserted Village.*

The facts of Goldsmith's life are almost too well known to need recapitulation here. He was born in Pallas, across the Longford border, where his father was assistant Rector, and quite literally 'passing rich with forty pounds a year.' A few years after his birth the family moved to the somewhat better parish of Lissoy and it was here that the future poet gathered his first impressions of life, and scenes and incidents of his boyhood recur again and again in his works. Of his father he says that 'his education was above his fortune, and his generosity greater than his education,' so we have no reason to doubt the accuracy of the picture of him drawn in *The Deserted Village*:

> *A man he was to all the country dear*
> *And passing rich with forty pounds a year:*
> *Remote from towns he ran his godly race*
> *No o'er had changed nor wished to change his place;*
> *Unpractised he to fawn or seek for power*
> *With doctrines fashioned to the varying hour;*
> *For other aims his heart had learned to prize,*
> *More skilled to raise the wretched than to rise.*
> *His house was known to all the vagrant train,*
> *The long-remembered beggar was his guest,*
> *Whose beard descending swept his aged breast;*
> *The ruined spendthrift, now no longer proud*
> *Claimed kindred there and had his claims allowed;*
> *The broken soldier, kindly bade to stay*
> *Sat by his fire and talked the night away,*
> *Wept o'er his wounds or tales of sorrow done.*
> *Shouldered his crutch and showed how fields were won.*

In *The Vicar of Wakefield*, Goldsmith's most famous prose work, his father is again the prototype, so we can readily believe that the real Vicar did not hedge himself in with those barriers of class and creed which separated the richer Anglo-Irish of those days from the people. The boy Goldsmith learned his alphabet at home and then proceeded to the village school, kept by one Thomas Byrne, or Paddy Byrne, who was an old soldier of Queen Anne's wars. His portrait is painted for us in the passage so well known:

> *A man severe he was and stern to view,*
> *I knew him well and every truant knew.*

But we are not told in the poem what we learn from other sources, that Paddy was a poet and Gaelic scholar. In this connection we may observe here that at the general loss of patronage which followed the breaking up of Irish civilisation at Kinsale and later at the Boyne, the poets adopted many callings to provide them with daily bread, while they wrote their dreams and visions for their own pleasure and the consolation of a vanquished people. Many of them turned schoolmasters, some became innkeepers, tenant farmers, or labourers, while many were among the soldiers of fortune who laid their arms at the service of every country in the war-racked Europe of the seventeenth and eighteenth centuries. They led wandering and often rather disreputable lives – not unlike Goldsmith himself – but they were always held in awed respect on account not only of their learning but of their withering powers of satire.

Paddy Byrne is in this tradition. We know that he translated Virgil into Irish verse, and that he had a profound knowledge of Gaelic literature and a fund of stories of his own adventures abroad and of the Raparees of his youth. Of his learning, the poem tell us:

> *The village all declared how much he knew,*
> *'Twas certain he could write and cypher too.*
> *Lands he could measure, terms and tides presage,*
> *And even, the story ran, that he could gauge.*

How very like is this passage to an extract from an actual advertisement written in Irish and English by another poet-schoolmaster of half a century later – the great Eoghan Ruadh O Sullivan of Muskerry. Asking for pupils for the school he is about to open, he says:

> *I'll engage*
> *To forward them with speed and care*
> *With Book-keeping and Mensuration,*
> *Euclid's Elements and Navigation,*
> *With Trigonometry and sound Gauging*
> *And English Grammar with rhyme and reason.*

This 'Eoghan Ruadh' too spent some time in the British Army. It must be remembered that after the Treaty of Limerick and the flight of the first Wild Geese, less than forty years before Goldsmith's birth, there was a constant exodus of young men from Ireland to the Continent – some to study for the Priesthood and others to join the Irish Brigades in the French and other armies. We know that Goldsmith learned to speak French fluently from the local Catholic Priest, and his knowledge of French literature shows itself in incidents in his works borrowed from earlier French writers. The battle of Ramilles was fought only twenty years before Goldsmith's birth, so we may reasonably suppose that some of the 'broken soldiers' who 'talked the night away' in the rectory kitchen had stories of 'that blood field' where after

> *The baffled French were forced to yield*
> *The victor Saxon backward reeled*
> *Before the charge of Clare's Dragoons.*

As the years went on, however, Irish boys began to join the army of the 'victor Saxon' when the link with the Continent was wearing thin, and there were few resources open to them at home. Thus Paddy Byrne in 1739 was not altogether an exception among old soldier-poets.

After Goldsmith had mastered what the village school had to teach him, he went to various other schools and finally entered Trinity College as a kind of poor scholar. His elder brother was already a Divinity student there, but poor Oliver showed no love or learning – in fact he was regarded as a waster and a dunce. He was constantly hard up, constantly being embroiled in some escapade or other, and often falling foul of his rather brutal tutor. He supplemented his slender allowance by writing ballad sheets at five shillings each for a Dublin publisher and used to steal out into the streets at night to hear them sung. He also appealed rather frequently to his generous uncle, the Rev. Thomas Contarine. However, at the age of twenty-one he succeeded in taking his B.A. degree and then came two years of glorious idleness at home, while he made up his mind what career he should choose. He fished in the Inny, hunted for otter, and lounged around Conway's public house in Ballymahon, and other inns there and in Lissoy, renewing old acquaintances and coming across such characters as Dick Muggins, the excise man, and Jack Slang, the horse doctor, whom Tony Tumpkin refers to as the high company of the Three Jolly Pigeons in *She Stoops to Conquer*. The plot of that famous comedy, by the way, is based on an actual incident of Goldsmith's youth. He was returning home for holidays, and, mounted on a borrowed horse and with a borrowed guinea in his pocket, he determined to put up for the night at an inn in Ardagh, like a gentleman. A local wag of whom he inquired the way to "the best house", directed him to the residence of Mr Featherstone, the local squire, who was enough of a humorist to keep up the joke, and it was only at his departure next morning that the embarrassed boy realised to whom he had been giving his peremptory and patronizing orders.

During these two years, Goldsmith made several false starts towards a career. First he presented himself as a candidate for Orders to the Bishop of Elphin, dressed in most unclerical scarlet breeches, and was refused, greatly to his relief. Later his kind uncle fitted him out with money and a horse to go to Cork, en route for America, but he returned without the money, riding a miserable nag which he very appropriately named 'Fiddleback.' An effort to reach the law school in London was no more successful – this time it was card-sharpers on the way to Dublin – but finally he did actually leave to study medicine at Edinburgh, and what is more, he actually arrived there. Thus he left his country at the age of twenty-four, and according to most of his biographers he never returned.

We will not follow the rest of his career in any detail. We know he tramped Europe with a flute (playing perhaps Carolan's reels and planxties) and obtained a medical degree somewhere on the way;

that he came to London and tried many occupations, and only drifted into literature by the accident of having to work for a time as a hack-reviewer of books for a London magazine. He was thirty-seven when *The Vicar of Wakefield* was published, and *The Deserted Village* did not appear till five years later. Nevertheless, he rapidly acquired fame and was looked up to as a master of literature by the greatest of his contemporaries. He enjoyed the generous friendship of the great Dr Johnson himself, and it is perhaps no one's fault but his own that he died in poverty at the early age of forty-six.

At this stage we may pause to consider the main criticisms levelled at Goldsmith's works. Many English critics, notably Lord Macaulay, take the view that in *The Deserted Village*, Auburn in its prosperity is not an Irish village at all, that the scene must have been drawn from Kent, the garden of England, for in the Ireland of the Penal Days no such prosperous community could possibly exist. It is a naïve comment surely from the compatriots of our benevolent rulers. William Black, speaking of this view, holds that 'while plausible it is unsound, for it happens to overlook one of the radical facts of human nature – the magnifying delight of the mind in what is long-remembered and remote.' Lissoy may have been a poor enough village, but viewed from his dreary garret in Fleet Street Court, it must have seemed to Goldsmith an earthly paradise. The elements of the picture are all to be found in any eighteenth century village:

> *The sheltered cot, the cultivated farm,*
> *The never-failing brook, the busy mill,*
> *The decent church that topped the neighbouring hill,*
> *The hawthorn bush with seats beneath the shade.*
> *For talking age and whispering lovers made.*

Goldsmith never had any intimate knowledge of English village life and he was notably unable to write from pure imagination; therefore it seems certain that when he sat down to describe a happy village, the Lissoy of his youth was before his mind. Undoubtedly he touched up the picture, as all artists do; he heightened the highlights and softened out the shadows. Some of our so called 'realists' of to-day would have given us the brawls and lurid language of the tavern, and turned the pool where the geese gabbled, into a stagnant cesspool, but their picture while much less pleasant would be no more true.

The second serious criticism is made by Irish commentators, that Goldsmith is not an Irish poet at all; that he wrote in the English mode for English readers. That also is a narrow view. Certainly it is true that, in name, the scenes of most of his works are laid in England. In *The Deserted Village* he seems to be tilting chiefly at a change in England's economic system:

> *A time there was ere England's griefs began,*
> *When every rood of ground maintained its man,*
> *And then in later years when the change came:*
> *The man of wealth and pride*
> *Takes up a space that many poor supplied;*
> *Space for his lake, his park's extended bounds;*
> *Space for his horses, equipage and hounds;*
> *The robe that wraps his limbs in silken sloth*
> *Has robbed the neighbouring fields of half their growth;*
> *His seat, where solitary sports are seen,*
> *Indignant spurns the cottage from the green.*

If that change occurred in England, it was not accompanied by half the cruelty and tyranny so familiar in Ireland, where

> *Trembling, shrinking from the spoiler's hand,*
> *Far, far away, thy children leave the land.*

The scene where the exiles 'fondly looked their last' at their old home; 'returned and wept and still returned to weep' is surely an Irish scene. Why then did Goldsmith not say so? For a very good reason. He lived in England and wrote for his daily bread at a time when to criticise England's policy in Ireland might have very serious consequences. Only a short time before, the author of *Robinson Crusoe* had his ears cut off for a pamphlet against the church party, in which he referred to one of the royal family as 'a fat Adonis of forty.' It is easy for us to be brave in these days of freedom of speech, but few of us in Goldsmith's day would have shown his temerity. In *The Traveller*, dedicated to his brother, he says

> *Have we not seen at pleasure's lordly call,*
> *The smiling, long frequented village fall?*

which should have shown to discerning readers that he was referring to what he and his brother had actually seen in Westmeath.

Irish poets writing in their native language in those times dared not mention their country's name or denounce England and English rule, except in the language of allegory. Thus Ireland is the lonely maiden whose spouse is far away, and England is the thief who stole the rich nourishing food from the family store. In Scotland for many years after the downfall of the Stuarts, the toast of 'the king over the water' was given secretly and silently by holding the glass over a tumbler of water at the dinner table.

Carolan the great harper, composed songs in praise of his friends and patrons, but never a word did he write about Ireland. We revere him as a great Irish poet, musician and composer, and yet we are hard on poor Goldsmith, who really did sing of his country and of her joys and sorrows in his own way.

As regards his turns of expression and poetic form, Goldsmith naturally used the style, metre and poetic diction universal in his day. His style is singularly natural and unaffected, but he can hardly be expected to avoid altogether the 'swains' and 'bowers' and 'arbors' and even the nightingales that formed the stock-in-trade of eighteenth century poetry. That unfortunate introduction of the nightingale to the Westmeath woods is, in my opinion, no more than that: the usual poetic sort of bird that sounded better than a robin or a sparrow. The days of Kiltartan English and 'the mist that does be on the bog' were still far off; the English reading public had not yet discovered the charm of the Celtic twilight; it was a far cry to the Gaelic revival of the late nineteenth century. So Goldsmith wrote English as it was written then, but behind the words 'the heart untravelled fondly turned to home.'

There is, by the way, a local tradition that Goldsmith did pay a visit to his brother after his wanderings in Europe, and that it was in Lissoy he wrote a great part of *The Deserted Village*, so that when he says 'And many a year elapsed return to view/Where once the cottage stood, the hawthorn grew,' he was really looking at the scenes of desolation he described. Local authorities give us the actual names of the original benign landlord and of the tyrant who replaced him, and usually local authorities are more reliable than literary critics far off.

Goldsmith then was Irish in that his character was formed in Ireland and that all through his life he looked back to Ireland with hopes 'here to return and die at home at last.' Yet Ireland has not treated his memory fairly. In his own words,

> *The very spot*
> *Where many a time he triumphed is forgot.*

His old home is in ruin, not even a road-sign shows the traveller the way up that neglected avenue.

If we today have done something to keep his memory alive we have done something worth while doing, and perhaps the day will come when some material monument will be erected bearing such an epitaph as that written to his memory by Robert Watt (compiler of the massive bibliography *Bibliotheca Britannica*):

Reader, if numbered in the Muse's train
Go, tune thy lyre, and imitate his strain;
But, if no poet thou, reverse the plan,
Depart in peace and imitate the man.

Francis Ledwidge

Lecture delivered at the Folk School in Bettystown, 1966. Margaret Conway lectured on Ledwidge on other occasions, notably in Slane in 1974 at the launch of Alice Curtayne's biography *Francis Ledwidge, A Life of the Poet* in which the author acknowledges her help, among that of other friends. Margaret Conway remembered meeting the poet when she was a young girl in Colga, when he visited her brothers and "fellow poets" at their home. Her painting of the Maiden Tower at Mornington, reproduced on the cover of this booklet, depicts a scene romantically associated with Francis Ledwidge and with Ellie, the young woman who inspired many of his poems.

Deirtear go bhfuil trí ní ná féidir iad a fhoghlaim: guth, féile agus filíocht. Pé aca fíor nó nach fíor é an sean-fhocal ina iomlán, is fíor é i dtaobh na filíochta de, i gcás Francis Ledwidge, an file atá mar adbhar cainte.

An old saying declares that there are three things that cannot be learned – a voice, generosity and the poetic gift. Whatever about the saying in general, it is certainly true with regard to the poetic gift in the case of Francis Ledwidge, the subject of this talk. Lord Dunsany wrote in 1914: "Neither in any class, nor in any country, nor in any age shall you predict the footfall of Pegasus, who touches the earth where he pleaseth, and is bridled by whom he will."

Does it sound pretentious? Pegasus descending on the Hill of Slane, to be bridled by a servant boy, son of a poor widow – one of a big family that had no access to the learning of the schools or the society of people educated in the classic tradition of Greek and Latin symbols – what would he know of Pegasus? But it was not extravagant. Ledwidge felt himself to be a poet. A friend of his has shown me an original letter in which he says he had written nothing lately, for "Pegasus is a fickle jade." In a poem about the Hounds he says of Fionn, "I who have the gift can hear Hounds and horns and tally-ho and the tongue of Bran as clear as Christmas bells across the snow."

But let's begin at the beginning. Francis Ledwidge was born in Slane in Co. Meath in 1888 and was killed in Flanders in the Summer of 1917 when he was 29 years of age. He went to school like every other child but he was fortunate that he had a very good master, a man called Madden, who, when he discovered that Frank was composing "rhymes," did not make fun of him.

We who have public libraries, radio and television, have no idea of the scarcity of books sixty-five years ago when Ledwidge was a boy of twelve with a thirst for book learning. The school readers of his elder brother, who was a monitor in the school, were almost his only source of literary material, and I suspect that it was in the old sixth book he first met Keats his first love and his first model. You probably know the poem he wrote at the age of 16, when he first left home and in his utter heartbroken loneliness saw Slane *Behind The Closed Eye*.

Note the lines:

> *And scenes of old again are born*
> *The woodbine lassoing the thorn*
> *And drooping Ruth like in the corn*
> *The poppies weep the dew*

If you had gone to school in the old days, as I did, you would have learned by heart the *Ode to the Nightingale*:

> *Perhaps that self same song had found a path.*
> *To the sad heart of Ruth, when sick for home*
> *She stood in tears amid the alien corn*

Beautiful to remember now, but to the twelve year old what drudgery to get it off by heart – (that was the easiest bit) – we could make no sense at all of the second verse:

> *Oh for a beaker full of the warm south*
> *Full of the true, the blushful Hippocrene*

But it all meant something to Ledwidge – the "dance and Provencal song and sunburnt mirth" intoxicated him, made him "half in love with easeful Death", so that long afterwards when again far away he wrote:

> *We'll fill a Provence bowl and pledge us deep*
> *The memory of the far ones, and between*
> *The soothing pipes, in heavy-lidded sleep*
> *Perhaps we'll dream the things that once have been*

If I dwell on his early years, I do so to show you what a poet is, and how he uses the tools that come to hand – what he observed, the birds the flowers the river, the little that he had read and the few metres he had heard – and this is something I have not yet resolved. Listen again to this first poem, *Behind The Closed Eye,* and see if you recall any poem that gave him the form :

> *I walk the old frequented ways*
> *That wind around the tangled braes,*
> *I live again the sunny days*
> *Ere I the city knew*

His contemporaries writing poems for the newspapers and for *Old Moore's Almanac* – for there were poets in every parish then – were on the level of "Way down a winding boreen in the bog of Ballymoney/ Stands a little whitewashed cabin with a weatherbeaten door", or the sort of patriotic ballad which was a copy of a copy of a copy of *Erin's isle my heart's delight.* Here was a child who had not just a poet's pen but a poet's eye to see the little things – the crane and the blackbird, the hawthorn and the woodbine, and, like Pearse, "the beauty of the world made him sad – this beauty that will pass." Ledwidge had not yet met Irish Ireland; he had not heard the name of Pearse; the Gaelic League was only beginning to spread into country places. He was to be much influenced by it later, but at this period literature to him meant English literature.

After his few weeks in Dublin, when he had left the shop he was working in and walked the thirty miles home, he lived like every other poor boy of his time, in any employment he could get – houseboy for a bit with a family that allowed him to read any book in their house, a great stroke of luck for him; then with local farmers; in the copper mine that was opened near Slane by the Lamberts; on the roads when direct labour came to Co. Meath. Early in the century he tried to form a Gaelic League branch (but got snubbed by the Navan people), and much later, in the days of Jim Larkin, the first labour union in rural Meath, and tried without success to get the secretaryship of the first National Health Insurance. Like every other young man, he danced and fell in love and went to the pub, and was so ordinary that the neighbours could not be convinced for many, many years that he was a poet – a real poet. But then, as all through his life, he was as it were two people – outwardly the ordinary or maybe rather odd young man, but inevitably and consciously the poet. Listen to this poem, written when he was in the British Army among tough soldiers, already having lived through horrors of war, and at the Dardanelles back in barracks in Derry. He had broken some of the rules, been drinking maybe and not returned to barracks; and he was court-martialled and sentenced to punitory detention.

This is what he wrote:

> *My mind is not my mind, therefore*
> *I take no heed of what men say,*
> *I lived ten thousand years before*
> *God cursed the town of Nineveh*
> (from *After Court Martial*)

And much earlier this one, *The Coming Poet*, which begins:

> *'Is it far to the town?' said the poet*
> *As he stood 'neath the groaning vane,*
> *And the warm lights shimmered silver*
> *On the skirts of the windy rain*

In those eight or nine years when he was working around home and had not yet met Lord Dunsany – that was 1912 – his best influence was probably the MacGoona family of Donaghmore, in the house at the Round Tower, a mile or so from An Uaimh, and some six or seven miles from Slane. I sat at that hospitable fireside a few days ago, in what Miss Winnie MacGoona told me was the Poet's Corner, and she told me how her brother Mattie and Frank sat one each side and talked half the night about all sorts of things, literature and nationality, religion and philosophy, life and death. They sang songs and they played music: Mattie was one of those who collected Irish music in those years. He was a compositor in the office of the *Irish Peasant* and as such was naturally involved in the very advanced ideas of W.P. Ryan. I think he greatly widened Ledwidge's horizons, as this poem, *To One Who Comes Now And Then*, shows:

> *…And sometimes from my shelf of poems you take*
> *And secret meanings to our hearts disclose,*
> *As when the winds of June the mid bush shake*
> *We see the hidden rose.*
> *And when the shadows muster, and each tree*
> *A moment flutters, full of shutting wings,*
> *You take the fiddle and mysteriously*
> *Wake wonders on the strings*

Note the simile of the little things – "the wind of June… each tree a moment flutters."

Then in 1912, Ledwidge sent a copybook full of poems to Lord Dunsany for his opinion on them. Dunsany, a man of letters himself, was discerning enough to see the merits of this young country boy in spite of flaws in grammar and even spelling. He tells us in his introduction to the first selection of poems how beautiful phrases leaped out from the pages,

> *In the red west the twisted moon is low*
> *And on the bubbles there are half lit stars*
> *Music and twilight; and the deep blue flow*
> *Of water, and the watching fire of Mars"*
> (from *Music on Water*)

or,

> *Within the oak a throb of pigeons wings*
> *Fell silent, and grey twilight hushed the fold*
> (from *A twilight in Middle March*)

and again – of Autumn,

> *And somewhere all the wandering birds are flown.*

or, in *After My Last Song*:

> *The air is smelling like a feast of wine*
> *And purple breakers of the sandy clover*
> *Shall roll to cool this burning brow of mine.*

"Why, this is how Meath looks," Dunsany says in his introduction to the first edition of *Songs of the Fields*. "It is just like that along the Boyne in April – quite taken by surprise by familiar things, for none of us knows, till the poets point them out, how many beautiful things are close about us."

Dunsany in his castle and Frank Ledwidge in his cottage – both were children of the Boyne Valley, and those of us privileged to live in Meath and to love the blue distances from our hills from Slane and Tara and the calm water at Stamullen and the woods of Beauparc, maybe, appreciate in a special kind of way "the blue distance is alive with song" or the final stanza of *To a Distant One*:

> *Your name is in the whisper of the woods …*
> *Oh when we meet there shall be sun and blue*
> *Strong as the Spring is strong*

Dunsany, of course, was in touch with the whole literary circle in Dublin (his uncle, Horace Plunkett, was concerned with A.E. Russell in the Co-operative movement) and it is to his eternal credit that he introduced this country boy to a circle which included Yeats, Joseph

Plunkett and Thomas MacDonagh. This was the beginning of a new life for Ledwidge. He may have had some acquaintance with stories from the Cattle Raid of Cooley from Standish O Grady's retelling or from Samuel Ferguson's poetry, but it was through his friendship with Thomas McDonagh that he came to know of poetry in Irish. It is doubtful if he could understand the poetry in the original, but McDonagh was at that time translating Irish poetry preserving the Irish mode, and, as you know, he published a volume dealing with the influence of Irish poetry on writers in English.

Have a look in *Fíon na Filíochta* at the poem which begins:

> *A bhonnáin bhuí, sé mo léan do luí*
> *is do chnámha sínte tar éis do ghrinn*

and at McDonagh's translation, "The yellow bittern that never broke out." Reading through Ledwidge's later poems we find him using the internal rhyme,

> *That love the springs of Bogac Ban*
> *Spread some new rumour round the dark*
> *And turned their faces from the dark dawn.*
> (from *Thro' Bogac Ban*)

or the poem *In France* written in wartime, in February 1917, the most perfect example is the lament for MacDonagh which we will come to later. He has themes from the Táin *(The Sorrow of Findebar)*

> *Beside the broad blue bend*
> *Of the slow river where the dark banks slope*
> *Wide to the woods sleep Ferdia apart*
> *I loved him, and then drove him for pride's sake*
> *To early death, and now I have no hope.*

and *The Death of Leag, Cuchulainn's Charioteer*:

> *By Nanny Water where the salty mists*
> *Weep oer Riángabra let me stand deep*
> *Beside my father.*

and from *An Fhiannaíocht* in *The Passing of Caoilte*:

> *And Caoilte the thin man, was weary now,*
> *And nodding in short sleeps of half a dream*
> *There came a golden barge down middle stream,*
> *And a tall maiden coloured like a bird*
> *Pulled noiseless oars, but not a word she said.*
> *And Caoilte, the thin man, raised up his head*
> *And took her kiss upon his throbbing brow,*
> *And where they went what man has heard.*

Of Ledwidge's life, apart from his poetry, from 1912-14, it is enough to say that he became, in the memory of his neighbours, very much the poet of fiction – long hair and flowing tie which to those who never saw nor even heard of A.E.'s beard or Yeats' ribbon, seemed a kind of madness.

In 1913, Ledwidge joined the Volunteers. By this time he was taking part in local affairs and by 1914 was a member of the Rural District Council. When John Redmond advised the Volunteers to join the British Army, Ledwidge was among the small number who remained loyal to Pearse. A month later he was taunted with being a Sinn Feiner at the R.D.C. meeting – the suggestion being made that the Irish Volunteers were men too cowardly to fight for small nations.

He showed plenty of courage in his answers to the 'loyal' members – and then quite inexplicably, walked out from the meeting and joined the Enniskillen Fusiliers – the 5th Battalion in which Lord Dunsany was a captain. Those interested in Ledwidge have argued much about his motives. Sufficient to say here that it was a time of much confusion of mind. There was the natural antipathy, on the

part of the ordinary people, to the English side in any war; against
that was a sort of romantic attachment to France: "King Louis
was loved by the Irish Brigade." There were men like Tom Kettle
– whom Ledwidge probably knew or at least knew of – poets, and
patriots apparently, on the recruiting platforms; there was the sense
of frustration perhaps, and it is said that 'Eilis of the Golden Hair'
had just turned him down – though he wrote to her frequently from
the army later on, and addressed poems to her. One could say that
at twenty-five he was singularly immature – very much the child in
matters of emotion, with a child's generosity and with little idea of
what the war was all about or of the horrors he would encounter.
It is fair to say that Lord Dunsany did not influence him directly,
though the fact that his patron to whom he looked up so much,
had already joined up, must have weighed with him – in so far as he
weighed things at all.

It would be tedious to follow his army career in any detail. Soon he
was in the force that landed at the Dardanelles and the first hand
accounts of that disastrous blunder which I have read reveal such
horrors for the men involved that they do not bear telling. But
through it all Ledwidge wrote at every odd minute back in billet on
any odd scrap of paper – about Slane and the blackbirds and the
fairy people and the things he knew and loved from childhood, as if
the war was not happening around him: he was as I have said before,
two people – the lance corporal and the king of Babylon.

Never a line about guns or shells or mangled men or the mud and
the thirst, but this:

> *The sheep are coming home in Greece,*
> *Hark the bells on every hill!*
> *Flock by flock, and fleece by fleece,*
> *Wandering wide a little piece*
> (from *The Home coming of the Sheep*)

or the poem *Evening Clouds.* In another poem he says:

> *Whatever way I turn I find the path is old unto me still*
> *The hills of home are in my mind and there I wander as I will*

and it was on active service he wrote the well known *Shadow People.*

Easter 1916 he was due home on leave. He got to England but there was no sailing to Dublin. One story says he managed to get to Ireland somehow but he certainly never reached Slane. An Irish journalist friend met him in Manchester during the following week and has given a description of his despair when he heard of the Rising and of the execution of his friends and fellow poets. During the fifteen months of life that were left to him he wrote many poems of lament for the poets, and poems explaining his own position, justifying himself in a way, but more and more expressing his loneliness. The most revealing perhaps is called *Ireland* . But perhaps the saddest is the *Dead Kings*. Note the wonderful last line: "I woke, 'twas day in Picardy."

The one sonnet I know (*Sonnet on some stones Lord Dunsany brought me from Sahara*) which was written much earlier, has wonderful last lines reminiscent of Keats:

> *And fear of children on the burning shore*
> *When Moses made a laneway in the sea*

But of all his Easter Week poems, the best known is the lament for Thomas MacDonagh. It is, in my opinion, one of the half dozen perfect lyrics in the English language – twelve lines in what MacDonagh had called the Irish mode. You are all familiar with it I am sure: it begins with the line "He shall not hear the bittern cry." *The Yellow Bittern (An Bonnán buí)* was in Ledwidge's mind. So was another poem which he knew in some translation, perhaps MacDonagh's own, *An Druimfhinn Donn dílis*, "the silk of the kine"

96

returning from the hills and misty valleys "to lift her horn in pleasant meads."

Three years ago the Slane Guild of Muntir na Tíre erected a plaque in memory of Ledwidge on the Bridge of Slane, a simple plaque beautifully designed by Seamas Murphy with Ledwidge's name and dates, 1889 – 1917.

> *He shall not hear the bittern cry*
> *In the wild sky where he is lain*

How appropriate it was for a man that wrote this, a few days before a sniper's bullet ended his short life:

> *This is a song a robin sang*
> *This morning on a broken tree*
> *It was about the little fields*
> *That call across the world to me*

Farther he is from the bittern and the robin and the blackbird in his unknown grave – Flanders – than is McDonagh in the quickline of Arbor Hill.

Perhaps I should finish there: but of all the poems I would love to read, I chose just one – the poet's testament one might call it – *The Deam of Artemis,* written just before the war, that begins:

> *There was soft beauty on the linnet's tongue*
> *To see the rainbow's coloured bands arch wide*

and this, towards the end:

> *I have not loved on Earth the strife for gold,*
> *Nor the great name that makes immortal man,*
> *But all that struggle upward to behold*

What still is left of beauty undisgraced,
The snowdrop at the heel of winter cold
And shivering, and the wayward cuckoo chased
By lingering March, and, in the thunder's van
The poor lambs marry on the meagre wold,
By-ways and cast-off things that lie therein,
Old boots that trod the highways of the world,
The schoolboy's broken hoop, the battered bin
The ragman's story, the blackened places
Where gypsies camped and circuses made din,
Fast water and the melancholy traces
Of sea tides, and poor people madly whirled
Up, down, and through the black retreats of sin.
These things a god might love, and stooping bless
With benedictions of eternal song.

The poems referred to in this lecture may be found in any edition of Ledwidge's complete works. The references here are taken from *The Complete Poems of Francis Ledwidge* with introductions by Lord Dunsany (London: Herbert Jenkins Limited Third edition 1955, first published 1919). Alice Curtayne's *Francis Ledwidge, A life of the Poet* (Dublin: Martin Brian and O'Keefe Ltd 1972) has been reprinted with an introduction by Jennifer Johnston by New Island Books, Dublin (1998) which has also published *Francis Ledwidge Selected Poems,* introduced by Seamus Heaney and edited by Dermot Bolger (2007).

Cuimhneachán an Athar Eoin

Is minic a thug Maighread Uí Chonmhidhe leachtai as Gaeilge, agus tá morchuid aca bailithe ag Meadhbh. Seo oráid a thug si ar ocáid speisialta – in Ath Bui i 1963 ag Cuimhneachán an Athar Eoin O Gramhnaigh, céad blian taréis a bháis.

Dá mbeadh an tAthair Ó Gramhnaigh ina bheathaidh inniu, ní fheadar cad a cheapfadh sé den Chuimhneachán Céid atá ar siúl againn i mbliana?

Ceapaim, ar an gcéad dul síos, go mbeadh ionadh air gur fiú linn a leithéid a bheith ar siúl againn in aon chor, mar ní raibh puinn measa aige ar a pháirt féin in obair na Gaeilge; is do dhaoine eile a thugadh sé an moladh i gcónaí. Ag tagairt do na daoine a d'doibrigh ar son na tíre agus ar son na teanga sna laethanta a bhí thart, dúirt sé: "Nuair a thiocfas lá na bua, i lár áthais, ríméid agus lúcháire an lae, déarfar an urnaí agus silfear an deoir ar son na laoch san uaigh; agus san am úd na Saoirse atá ag druidim in aice linn, beidh aos óg na tíre ag tabhairt turas ar leapacha déanacha na ngaiscíoch a throid an troid mhaith, agus ag deargadh ansin lasrach an tírghrá ina gcroí." Ar na gaiscígh úd, níl duine ba mhó a thuill an urnaí agus an deoir ná é féin. Ach bhí sé ró-umhal é féin a áireamh ina measc.

Bheadh, leis, áthas ar an Athair Eoin go bhfuil an tSaoirse tagtha: go bhfuil meas ar an gcine Gael i measc na náisiún; go bhfuil deireadh leis an mbochtanas agus leis an tarcaisne a leanann é; go bhfuil an Ghaeilge á múineadh i scoileanna na hÉireann; go bhfuil an oiread leabhar á gcur i gclo agus an oiread litríochta den chéad scoth á scríobh inti.

Ach mar sin féin, bheadh iarracht de dhíomá air, leis. Sa leabhrán seo, is i mBéarla atá an phríomhchuid dá bheathaisnéis, mar d'ainneoin seachtó bliain de shaothar ó bunaíodh Conradh na Gaeilge, agus daichead bliain d'fhéinrialtas, tá formhór de mhuintir na tíre nach dtuigfeadh alt as Gaeilge, agus faraoir, cuid mhaith acu nach dtrialfadh í a léamh ná í a thuiscint.

Nuair a bhí an tAthair Eoin ag fáil bháis i bhfad óna thír agus óna mhuintir, tar éis a neart agus a shláinte a ídiú i seirbhis na teanga, b'é an sólás ba mhó a bhí aige ná go raibh toradh ar an íobairt – go raibh an Ghaeilge slán. B'shin mar a cheap mórán daoine nach é; is fiú nuachtáin an ama a léamh agus iad ag cur síos ar an athrú a bhí tagtha; deireadh leis an ndrochmheas, náire ar dhaoine a admháil nach raibh aon Ghaeilge acu, agus mar sin de. "Is mór í an Fhírinne agus tiocfaidh sí in uachtar," arsan tAthair Seán O Raghallaigh, ag labhairt ins an tsochraid i Má Nuat. "Ba fhírinne ann féin an tAthair Eoin, agus tá leis anocht ar talamh chomh maith agus ar neamh."

"Deich mbliana ó shin," arsan tAthair Peadar O Laoghaire, bhí an Ghaeilge chomh himithe sin nach raibh aon tsúil ag éinne go bhféadfaí í a choimeád beo... Na daoine nach raibh aon fhocal di ina mbéal acu, bhí móráil orthu mar gheall air. Na daoine go raibh sí acu, ní admhóidis é. Ansin is ea a chuir Dia i gcroí an tsagairt sin go bhfuil a chnámha ansin sínte os ár gcomhair anocht, éirí agus aghaidh a thabhairt ar an nGaeilge agus í á saothrú agus gan ligint di dul ar fad as an saol. Táimid cruinnithe anocht chun onóra a thabhairt dó mar gheall ar an obair a dhein sé, agus chun onóir a thabhairt do Dhia na Glóire a chuir ina chroí an obair a dhéanamh."

Go ceann fiche bliain lean gluaiseacht na Gaeilge, agus chuir anáil faoi gach gluaiseacht fónta sa tír: drámaíocht, litríocht, ceol, cluichí, ealaíon. An mórtas a chuir sí sna daoine is é a mharaigh an tÉireannach stáitse: is é a choimeád amach mórchuid de na hamhráin gháirsiúla ghallda; is é a chabhraigh fiú le measarthacht san ólachán. Éinne a bhí ina bhall de Chonradh na Gaeilge sna laetheanta úd, nó éinne a dhein freastal ar cheann de na Coláistí Samhraidh, is cuimhin leis an sonas agus an t-aoibhneas agus an draíocht a bhain leis an ngluaiseacht. Is deacair iad a chur i bhfocail. B'fhéidir nár fhoghlaim cuid de na mic léinn an oiread gramadaí agus filíochta is a bhainfeadh amach an Mhéanteist dóibh inniu. Ach ba phéarla thar luach leo gach seanrá amach as béal cainteora ó dhúchas, agus nuair a chanadar 'Fáinne Geal an Lae', chonacadar na soilse ag teacht, agus d'airíodar Cáit Ní Dhuibhir ag glaoch ar chlann na Gaeilge. Go deo arís, ní bheidís gafa ar fad le leathphingne smearacha an tsaoil.

B'iad Clann na Gaeilge a bhain amach an tsaoirse shaolta atá againn. Ach cad a tharla don tsaoirse spioradálta? Ar imigh Ré na nAislingí i 1921? Ní hé seo an áit an cheist a phlé, agus ní fheileann éadóchas don ócáid. B'fhearr an sliocht seo a leanas a chur síos mar ábhar machnaimh do Ghaeilgeoirí na linne seo. Is é an tAthair Donncha O Floinn, Comharba an Athar O Gramhnaigh i gColáiste Mhá Nuat, a labhair é, an lá ar nochtadh an leacht Cuimhneacháin in Áth Buí i 1956:

"Ní ceart dúinn ár súile a chaochadh ar na mílte de dhaoine óga a fhágann ár scoileanna gach bliain, agus i bhfad ó aon ghrá a bheith acu do na nithe ba ghreann leis an Athair Eoin, gur gráin a bhíonn acu orthu... Nach bhfuil sé glan le feiscint, má bhíonn an dearcadh mínádurtha sin ag a lán dár n-aos óg, ag teacht amach dóibh as na scoileanna atá in ainm a bheith bunaithe ar ídéalacha Uí Ghramhnaigh... go bhfuil alt éigin fágtha ar lár againn as a theagasc; óir b'é Eoin O Gramhnaigh aspal an ghrá ar Éirinn agus ar ar bhain léi.

Agus sin é díreach an leigheas. Níl aos óg an lae inniu aon phioc níos stuacaí ná níos dúire ná níos leisciúla ná aon ghlún dá ndeaghaidh rompu; ach iarrann siad ídéalacha, iarrann siad fís; agus "san áit nach mbíonn fís le fáil, gheibheann an pobal bás."

Iarraimis ar Dhia na Glóire sa bhliain seo 1963, Bliain Uí Ghramhnaigh, "an lasrach a dheargadh" inár gcroí agus ár súile a oscailt don fhís úd a bhí i gceist ag Comharba Uí Ghramhnaigh – an Náisiún Gaelach a thógáil le bheith ina eiseamláir don domhan ar cad is náisiún Críostaí ann.

AN GHAEILGE LE'N ÁR LINN

Cur síos ar thaithí Mhaighréad Uí Chonmhidhe ó thús an 20ú haois, i gContae Lú, i mBaile Átha Cliath agus i gContae na Mí. Tá taithí a fir céile luaite chomh maith. Is do Mháire Brück, a hiníon, a scríobh sí an cuntas sin mar chúlra do léacht a bhí le tabhairt aici i nDún Éidinn i 1968.

Níor leath Conradh na Gaeilge ar fuaid na tíre i gceart go dtí 1900. Go dtí sin, ó bunaíodh í in 1893, bhí a lán daoine ag cur spéise ann agus ag leanúint na gceachtanna beaga Gaeilge ins na páipéir sheachtainiúla, agus cuid acu ag ceannach *Irisleabhar na Gaeilge;* ach lucht léinn ba ea iad siúd – múinteoirí scoile, sagairt óga, céimithe agus fodhaoine eile tuisceanacha – daoine b'fhéidir go raibh traidisiún na bhFíníní acu.

Ach nuair a leath scéala bhás an Athair Uí Ghramhnaigh do chuaigh sé go croí gnáthdhaoine ar a shon gur sagart é, agus go raibh sé óg agus gurb é a chuid oibre ar son na Gaeilge a bhris a shláinte. Ba ghearr go raibh craobhacha ins geall le gach paróiste sa tír.

Tá leabhar Uí Ghramhnaigh Cuid a I anseo againn, ainm Thomáis Uí Chonmhidhe air, fén dáta 1901. Ba é Micheál O Floinn a thosaigh an craobh i Maigh Dearmhaí ag an am sin. Fear óg é a raibh siopa aige sa tsráid, ach fear go raibh an-chuid léite aige, agus a bhí ó nádúr, acadúil. Bhí sé tamall ag gabháil don Ghaeilge, ní foláir, mar is gearr go raibh sé ina scoláire, agus aithne aige ar dhaoine mar Sheán T. (O Ceallaigh) agus fiú an Craoibhín féin. Bhí daoine mar é níos coitianta sa tír ná mar a bheifí ag súil leis. Ní raibh aon mhúinteoir acu ar dtús, ach do bhailigh siad beagán airgid chun roinnt ceachtanna a fháil ó sheanfhear ó Chiarraí a bhí ina chónaí i mBaile Átha Troim (O Drisceoil) agus ceapaim go raibh sé ar pinsean ós na póilíní. Bhí cuid mhaith de mhuintir an pharóiste sa rang, buachaillí óga ba mhó a bhí cheana sa Chumann Iománaíochta. Ba shin mar a bhí i ngach áit – mar shampla bhí aeraíocht in mBaile Átha Troim 1902 inar labhair Pádraig Mac Piarais, agus bhí baint ag na hiománaithe leis. (San Uaimh bhí Cuimhneacháin '98 ar Chnoc na Teamhrach 1898, agus dúirt Seán Mac Fhearghaill, iarchathaoirleach ar Comhairle Contae na Mí, liom gur ag deireadh an lae sin a bunaíodh Craobh na hUaimhe – bhí sé féin ann agus gan ann ach garsún.)

Bhí an chéad Fheis sa Mhí i 1904, agus do bhuaigh Tomás O Conmhidhe duaiseanna ann. Bhí buachaill de mhuintir Vaughan, an gabha, as an tsráidbhaile, a chuaigh ag obair sa Longphort agus ón tosach a bhí déanta aige sa bhaile do lean sé agus bhuaigh sé, nó bhí sé i gcomórtas ar aon chuma, san Oireachtas níos déanaí.

Ach ar an iomlán níor fhoghlaim na gnáthdhaoine mórán. Ní raibh éirim aigne nó an fonn staidéir acu. Ach bhí siad an-mhórálach as an mbeagán a bhí acu, agus ceapaim gur lean spiorad na teanga iontu. Ba iad a bhí ins na hÓglaigh níos déanaí.

I gcionn tamaill leath múinteoirí taistil tríd an tír, agus ní dóigh liom go raibh aon tosach ar an nGaeilge inár bparóiste sa bhaile go dtí sin, mar is cuimhin liom an chéad oíche go raibh rang agus ní foláir nó go rabhas a sé nó a seacht – i 1905, b'fhéidir. Fear ón dúthaigh in aice Dún Dealgan a bhí ann – fear óg ach Gaeilge éigin aige ón gcliabhán – is dócha go raibh sé tar éis freastal ar ranganna i nDún Dealgan in éineacht le Peadar Ó Dubhda (atá fós ina bheathaidh – os cionn 90, déarfainn.)

Do bheadh rang oíche uair sa tseachtain agus rang leathuair an chloig ar scoil an lá céanna (scoileanna agus ranganna i bparóistí eile gach lá.) Ceapaim gur ag a trí a chlog a bhí cead é do mhúineadh mar "ábhar breise" (cosúil le cócaireacht) taobh amuigh de ghnáthamanna scoile agus gheobhadh an máistir táille (an duine) as gach leanbh go n-éireodh leis don chigire. Ach ní dóigh liom go raibh scrúdú riamh againn ag an am. Níor lean an múinteoir sin ró-fhada, agus ceapaim go raibh beirt nó triúr eile againn sula d'fhág mé i 1911. Ag tosú i gcónaí a bhíomar.

Do bhí rang Gaeilge againn in Ard Mhacha (Clochar an Chroí Ró-Naofa) – ní raibh an meas uirthi is a bhí ar an bhFraincis nó ar an nGearmáinis – dhá rang sa tseachtain, sa tráthnóna – cailín ón mbaile cuid den am, agus ansin cailín a bhí tar éis bheith ar scoil agus a dhein staidéar do chéim sheachtrach (extern) i gColáiste na

Tríonóide agus í ina cónaí sa scoil. (Máire Ní Ghaoithín – bhí sí ina cigire ina dhiaidh sin agus scrúdaigh sí i gCúl Rónáin uair éigin – tar éis 1930, ceapaim). Ní raibh ach 8-10 againn sa rang, ceapaim.

Ach ina dhiaidh sin nuair a bhíos i nDún Dealgan (1914-1918) – is sa scoil náisiúnta a bhíos – mar monitress, agus bhí an Ghaeilge mar ábhar breise acu, agus sinne dá déanamh don scrúdú iontrála (i gcóir Dún Chéire) mar ábhar breise leis. Bhí sí dá múineadh ag na Bráithre i ngach áit, agus is Graiméir leo a bhí in úsáid i ngach scoil. Téacs leis an Athair Peadar againn – do léimis os ard ach ní raibh aon chomhrá – ní raibh aon bhean rialta ábalta an Ghaeilge a labhairt. Do théadh cuid againn ar Chonradh na Gaeilge sa bhaile (1916 amach) ach ní go rómhaith a thaitin sé sin leis na mná rialta.

Tar éis 1916 tháinig borradh mór faoi Chonradh na Gaeilge i ngach áit. (Ceapaim go raibh sé tar éis dul síos le roinnt bliana roimhe sin.) Faoin am seo bhí an-fheabhas tagtha ar an modh múinte – comhrá ba mhó i gcónaí gan amhras – ach tháinig "an modh ráite" isteach – abairtí i bhfoirm agallaimh de glanmheabhair, tar éis iad d'úsáid agus do chasadh i ngach slí le linn an ranga. Ní bhíodh aon fhocal Béarla – fiú le daoine ag tosú, agus bhí cead acu siúd iad do scríobh síos de réir na bhfuaimeanna dá mba mhaith leo. Aon áit go raibh múinteoir maith bhí daoine ábalta labhairt go maith tar éis cúrsa gairid go leor.

In 1917 (ceapaim) do bunaíodh an Coláiste Gaeilge in Ó Méith – bhíos ann deireadh seachtaine nó dhó, ach i 1918 dheineas an mhí iomlán agus den chéad uair bhíos ábalta labhairt. Bhí sé go hiontach – daoine de gach aois, ó shlua leanaí faoi chúram Louise Gavin Duffy, go seandaoine mar W. P. Ryan, (an tAthair Desmond a scríobh stair 1916 etc.), sagairt, múinteoirí, intelligentia – iad go léir aerach – lán dáiríre gan amhras ach lán de spórt – Eoin Mac Néill mar dhuine de na léachtóirí. Suas an sliabh sa tráthnóna go dtí na seandaoine go raibh Gaeilge acu – bhí beagán ag cuid de na daoine óga – ceol, rincí, bádóireacht.

Ag an deireadh fuair mé féin agus W. P. Ryan teastas .i. go n-aithneofaí thú mar mhúinteoir Gaeilge i scoil (Bhí W. P. ag múineadh i gConradh na Gaeilge i Londain.) Bhí na Coláistí go léir mar a chéile – nó níos fearr, b'fhéidir – chuaigh Tomás Ó Conmhidhe go Béal Átha an Ghaorthaidh i 1909 – ní raibh an Coláiste ró-fhada ann roimhe sin – níl an dáta agam – agus bhí sé sa Daingean bliain eile. Ní raibh aon deontas acu faoi na Sasanaigh – dhíoladh gach duine £1 don chúrsa.

Nuair a bhí Tomás Ó Conmhidhe sa Choláiste i nDroim Conrach (1905-1907) bhí rang Gaeilge ann (ní raibh sé riachtanach freastal air) agus ba é Eoin Mac Néill an múinteoir cuid den am, agus ina dhiaidh sin Tadhg Ó Donncha (Torna). Mar a chéile nuair a bhíos i nDún Chéire (Carysfort) (1918 – 1920) ba é Donncha Ó Loinsigh ó Bhaile an Fheirtéaraigh an tOllamh; an-eolas aige ach níor mhúin sé faic – seanfhear a bhí ann ag an am – agus ní raibh aon mheas ar an rang. Ní bhíodh ach leath na mac léinn ann.

Ach bhí an-chuid den leath san an-láidir – agus bhíodh a lán argóintí ann. Ní raibh aon spéis ag an chuid is mó de na mná rialta ann – ach ní raibh mórán spéise acu ionainn ach chomh beag.

Taobh amuigh bhí na ranganna ag dul i méid de réir mar a bhí ag géarú ar an troid. Do bunaíodh Coláiste Leanaí i gCeann Clochair i samhradh 1920 – do mhúineas ann ar feadh trí seachtaine (seantig cinn tuí agus cúpla bothán adhmaid) – 50 leanbh, buachaillí agus cailíní, ó 5 bliain go 15 – leanaí Art Uí Gríobha orthu.

As san go dtí an Sos Comhraic (samhradh 1921) bhíos i mBaile Átha Cliath – bhí na ranganna go hiontach, ach b'éigin iad do chiorrú ar dtús agus ansin iad do dhúnadh síos ar fad toisc an Curfew. Bhíodar go hiontach arís le linn na bliana ina dhiaidh sin sular thosaigh an scoil agus an Cogadh Cathartha (Meitheamh 1922).

D'ainneoin an 'scoilt' agus gach rud, do dhein an Rialtas nua cúrsaí do chur ar bun. Tugadh saoire bhreise do gach scoil in

Éirinn ar feadh roinnt blianta agus ceapaim gur lean na cúrsaí sé seachtaine. Do bhíos ag múineadh sa chéad ceann, i Sráid Maoilbhríde, agus is lena linn a thosaigh an troid – ag na Ceithre Chúirte san oíche – agus an chéad lá eile nuair a bhíomar istigh thosaigh sé i Sráid Uí Chonaill agus b'éigin dúinn siúl i bhfad i dtreo Marino chun teacht ar Shráid Berkeley, áit go raibh cúpla duine againn ar lóistín – ach tar éis seachtaine do leanamar leis an cúrsa arís. Daoine ag tosú is mó a bhí agamsa sa 'Bun-Rang' – mná aosta ab ea cuid acu, agus do thriail mé iad do mhúineadh sa tslí ba cheart dóibh féin na leanaí óga do mhúineadh. Bhí ranganna den saghas céanna ar siúl ins na bailte – An Muileann gCearr, An Uaimh, agus a leithéid. Chuaigh Tomás Ó Conmhidhe an bhliain sin ar choláiste i mBrí Chualainn (Bré) ina raibh ard-ranganna speisialta, agus an chéad bhliain eile chuaigh sé go Baile Mhúirne agus fuair sé Ard-Teastas (rud nua). Níor chuas féin in aon áit i 1923 mar fuair m'athair bás ag tús an tsamhraidh. Tháinig mé go Baile Íomhair sa bhfómhar. Sa bhliain 1924 dheineas an tArd-Teastas i mBaile Mhúirne, agus chuaigh Tomás ag múineadh ag an gcúrsa i nDroichead Átha, agus lean sé de gach samhradh go dtí gur cuireadh deireadh leo (ceapaim) i 1928. Ina dhiaidh sin bhíodh fós cúrsaí ins na coláistí sa Ghaeltacht go ceann i bhfad. Ceapaim go rabhamar i gCúil Aodha 1929, 1932, 1933 (tá cúrsaí fós ann, ceapaim, ach rudaí speisialta ar an dul céanna le cúrsaí léinn eile).

Ins na blianta san leis bhí mórán cúrsaí beaga príobháideacha ins na hoícheanta geimhridh ag múinteoirí, státseirbhísigh. (Agus ag gardaí, ach níl fhios agam an raibh siadsan "oifigiúil" – bhíodh Donncha Ó Meachair, múinteoir le Conradh na Gaeilge, ag múineadh na ngardaí i mBaile Íomhair tamaill).

Chomh fada is is cuimhin liom anois do chuaigh Conradh na Gaeilge síos ins na blianta sin ar fad – bhí an scoilt i ngach paróiste, agus gach aoinne an-searbh, ní nach ionadh. Nílim cinnte ar thosaigh ranganna Gaeilge oíche fé na seancheardscoileanna (techs) a bhí le blianta ins na bailte móra mar An Uaimh, Droichead Átha, Dún Dealgan, ach nuair a thosaigh na Gairm-scoileanna (Vocational

Education 1930) fé stiúir coistí ins gach contae, do bhí ranganna oíche aon áit go raibh éileamh orthu – mar a chéile le cócaireacht, adhmadóireacht – agus sa chontae seo ar aon chuma níor dhein na coistí aon rud chun iad do spreagadh – a mhalairt ar fad. Sa chontae seo, agus is dócha in a lán áiteanna eile, ba é Cumann na nGael a bhí i gceannas ar na coistí, agus ortha san bhí an-chuid sean-"daoine uaisle" (Lord Dunsany, Duc de Stacpoole) agus ar a laghad cléireach amháin Caitliceach agus duine eile Protastúnach. Chomh maith leis san bhí rud éigin le síniú ag gach múinteoir – geallúint bheith dílis don Rialtas – agus is toisc ná síneodh sé é go raibh Dónall Ó Cuinn ar an seachrán, agus do dhein Conradh na Gaeilge sa chontae (bhí sé ann i gcónaí cé nach raibh mórán ar siúl ach an Fheis gach bliain) sórt fo-choiste chun ranganna do chur ar siúl dó. Ba é Danny féin rúnaí an Chonradh sa chontae i bhfad roimhe sin, agus bhí baint éigin againn leis na feiseanna.

Caithfear a rá gur tháinig gach páirtí ar na ranganna i mBaile Íomhair. Tar éis an toghcháin áitiúil i 1934, bhí tromlach ag Fianna Fáil i ngach áit agus bhí deireadh leis an síniúchán. Sin é an t-am gur cuireadh mise (agus Pádraig Ó Luasaigh, beannacht Dé leis) ar an Choiste – b'éigean beirt mhúinteoirí bheith air, de réir dlí. Do lean ranganna oíche ach ní go ró-mhaith – an chigireacht cuid den chúis agus nach raibh an saoirse a bhíodh ag Conradh na Gaeilge – an chaint agus an ceoil – agus bhí cuid de na múinteoirí aosta agus gan aon mhaith iontu sa saol athraithe. Fén am san leis, toisc Gaeilge bheith ins na scoileanna, ní raibh fonn ar dhaoine óga é d'fhoghlaim arís san oíche.

Anois ceist na scoileanna náisiúnta agus na múinteoirí. Tá an-chuid difríochtaí. Múinteoirí chomh h-óg liomsa bhí roinnt Gaeilge acu cheana, mura rabhadar ina coinne ar fad. Fiú má bhí, nuair a bhí a fhios acu gurbh éigean dóibh í a mhúineadh bhíodar ábalta í a fhoghlaim. Daoine a bhí, abair 30, mura raibh spéis acu inti cheana, ní raibh sé chomh furasta orthu, ach aoinne acu a bhí in aon tslí cliste bhíodar ábalta tosú á múineadh slí éigin tar éis an chéad chúrsa agus bhíodar ag dul i bhfeabhas. (Sampla maith í Bean Mhic Oireachtaigh). Bhí cuid mhaith ag Mrs Dargan – chuaigh sí ar Choláiste Tuar Mhic Éidigh i 1911. Daoine níos mó ná 40 nó 50 bhí sé ró- chrua orthu, mar aoinne acu siúd nár dhein staidéir éigin air fé Chonradh na Gaeilge is léir ná raibh fonn staidéir orthu – cuid mhaith acu ní raibh go leor oideachais acu chun aon rud d'fhoghlaim – mar shampla na mná rialta a bhí meán-aosta, agus cuid acu ag múineadh cé ná raibh aon oideachas in aon chor acu, agus gur bhain a muintir leis an aicme is moille chun glacadh le smaointe nua – nó le haon smaointe in aon chor – feirmeoirí, siopadóirí agus a leithéid. (Bunscoileanna atá i gceist fós).

Bhí deacracht eile: na cigirí agus na státseirbhísigh. Nuair a ghlac an Rialtas cumhacht i 1922, bhí rogha fén gConradh (Article 10) ag aon státseirbhíseach dul ag obair sa tuaisceart nó i Sasana nó dul amach ar pinsean, ach d'fhan an chuid is mó acu. I gcás cigirí ba bheag acu go raibh aon Ghaeilge acu, agus bhí cúpla cúrsa samhraidh acu. Ach – toisc b'fhéidir ná raibh an teanga ar a dtoil acu – bhíodar an-chrua ag scrúdú na ndaltaí: Gramadach an t-aon rud a thuigeadar, agus aistriúchán. B'fhuath leo nós múinte Chonradh na Gaeilge (bog-Irish a thug duine acu uirthi ag scrúdú i mBaile Íomhair!) Do ceapadh roinnt cigirí óga, ach bhí an system ró-láidir dóibh. Bhíodar dian ar na múinteoirí ná raibh ach ag foghlaim agus do bhriseadar aon mhisneach a bhí acu; bhíodar dian orainne a bhí tar éis bheith ag múineadh go maith – cé nár éirigh leo buachaint orainn, b'éigean dúinn, mar sin féin, "cinn línte", deachtú etc. do dhéanamh, agus nótaí gan chiall ar an méid briathra agus díochlaonta agus gach diabhal rud a bhí déanta againn. Níor thuig aoinne acu conas teanga do mhúineadh. Is cuimhin liom ban-chigire, cailín macánta, a scrúdaigh sibh agus Eithne sa treas rang. Bhí sí ag féachaint an raibh an aimsir fháistineach ar eolas acu, agus pé slí a chuir sí an cheist ar cad a dhéanfaidís tar éis dul abhaile ón scoil an lá san, dúirt Eithne "Dul go dtí an siopa má bhíonn aon rud ag teastáil, agus ansan mo chuid tae d'ól etc. agus cad a dúirt an cigire liom? "Tá an cailín sin ró-ghlic: níl an Aimsir Fháistineach ar eolas aici, agus tá sí ag casadh an fhreagra. Lá eile bhí fear ag scrúdú agus cuir sé ceist "Cad a dhéanfá dá leanfadh mactíre thú?" Dúirt duine amháin "Rachainn suas crann." Dúirt mo dhuine "Muna mbeadh crann ann…?" agus dúirt leanbh eile "dul suas ar fhalla"– "ní hea", agus do thrialladar gach míle rud a bhí timpeall na háite – "isteach i dtig", "isteach san abhainn" etc. Ach is dóigh liom gur tusa (.i. Máire) féin a bhí glic go leor smaoineamh go raibh focal éigin in aigne an chigire agus dúirt tú "Dul isteach i bpluais". "Sea, sea," ar seisean, agus é an-sásta agus lean sé le ceisteanna ar phluaiseanna! Is dócha gurb shin an liosta ceisteanna agus freagraí a bhí scríofa síos aige!

Do lean iarsmaí an droch-thosnú ar feadh i bhfad – do dhein an scrúdú (Primary Cert) níos measa é, mar do bhí an béim go léir ar scríbhneoireacht. Ní ach anois atáid ag teacht ar ais go dtí ár slí-ne.

B'fhéidir gurb é an rud ab fhearr a dhein an Rialtas ins na blianta tosaigh ná na Coláistí Ullmhúcháin a bhunú i 1926. Bhí Seán Newman ar an gcéad dream, agus tá fhios agat a fheabhas is a bhí sé, agus Áine Ní Mhuireadhaigh trí bliana ina dhiaidh. De réir mar a thángadar san amach (agus de réir mar a deineadh cigirí de chuid acu) tháinig feabhas mór ar an scéal. (Tá deireadh leis na gcoláistí sin anois – is dócha nach bhfuil an gá céanna leo.)

Ón méid atá scríofa agam, cheapfadh duine nár éirigh in aon chóir leis na scoileanna agus ní fíor sin. Is éachtach an méid Gaeilge atá ar eolas ag daoine de gach saghas – cé ná labhraíonn siad í, agus cé go gceapann siad nach bhfuil aon chuid acu. Mura mbeadh na Bunscoileanna ní éireodh le méanscoileanna maithe mar Mhuineachán, nó fiú le hOllscoil na Gaillimhe. Tá Gaeilge an-mhaith ag an chuid is mó de na daoine go bhfuil postanna acu in aon seirbhís phoiblí – Rúnaí Chomhairle an Chontae, na cléirigh istigh, gan trácht ar phostanna níos airde, agus fé láthair tá an-chuid acu san a labhraíonn go nádúrtha liom í. Agus tá dream óg – aois Ultan – a úsáideann í ina gcuid gnó agus i rudaí mar Comhaltas Ceoltóirí etc.

Ach níos tábhachtaí fós, tá gach aoinne sa Ghaeltacht ábalta léamh as Gaeilge – rud ná raibh tríocha bliain ó shin, agus is astu siúd agus as Gaeilgeoirí i gcoitinne atá an litríocht agus na drámaí is fearr ag teacht – cuid acu mar *An Giaill* le Behan a aistríodh go Béarla (*The Hostage*) agus *An Triall* le Máire Ní Ghrádaigh. Tá an sean-litríocht á haistriú ag daoine mar David Marcus, Frank O'Conor, (beannacht Dé leis), Séamus Carney etc. agus omós dairíribh á thabhairt do Briain Mac Giolla Meidhre, Peadar Ó Doirnín, do scoláirí mar Daithí Ó hUaithne, Myles Dillon etc. – lucht logainmneacha – Daonscoil – *Réalt* etc. a scrúdáíonn ceisteanna ilghnéitheacha trí Ghaeilge. Tá leathdosaen nuachtán seachtainiúil agus míosúil ann (*Inniu, Feasta, Ultach, Rosc*, agus, *Amárach, Comhar*) Tá leabhar de gach saghas ón alán club leabhar – scéalta, stair, agus, mar shampla, *Stairí Mellifont ins na Meánaoiseanna* ag an Athair Colmcille atá ina mhanach i Mellifont nua. *An Sagart– Iris leabhar Magh Nuad.*

Dheineas dearmad cúrsaí samhraidh leanaí do lua. Tugann Feiseanna, ceardscoileanna etc. scoláireachtaí. (Coiste na bPáistí, chomh fada is eol dom is fé na gCeardchumainn é, agus ceapaim go bhfuil a leithéid de scéim ag na Gardaí agus ag an Arm). Bíonn gach áit lán sa samhradh – na cúrsaí i mBrú na Mí, St. Martha's, Warrenstown, agus a leithéid i gcontaetha eile agus gach uile Gaeltacht – coláistí móra curtha suas acu agus gach cóir orthu. Tá roinnt mhaith daoine a dhíolann astu féin. Bíonn deontas ón Roinn Oideachais ag na coláistí go léir. Tá an oiread daoine cliste ag scríobh nach féidir iad d'ainmniú – Seán Mac Réamoinn, Seán Ó Ríordáin, agus Máirtín Ó Cadhain.

Anois ceist na nGaeltachtaí sa Mhí. Arís, do dheineadh go holc é i dtosach. Bhí estáit móra dá roinnt ar fheirmeoirí bheaga ins gach áit ó 1923 (do deineadh beagán de sin fé na Sasanach) agus i gcónaí is iad na daoine mórthimpeall a gheibheadh píosaí. Bhí gcargá i gContae na Mí, mar toisc an méid feirmeacha an-mhóra, ó aimsir na 'clearances' bhí an-chuid daoine ins na portacha (Cuil Rónáin m.sh.) ar trí nó ceithre acra. Mar sin bhí an-éad leis na ndaoine a tháinig ón iarthar, agus cé gur chuireamar (Conradh na Gaeilge) fáilte 'oifigiúil' rompu, is beag comhluadar a dhein aoinne leo ina dhiaidh sin – ach troid idir iad agus na Midhigh ins na pubanna in Áth Buí. Ach do choimeádadar a gcuid Gaeilge, go mór mór i Ráth Cairn – a bhuíochas do Seán Ó Coisdealbha agus a bhean a bhí mar athair agus máthair dóibh. Do dhein daoine airithe an-díobháil i mBaile Ghib – ach tá sé maith go leor mar sin féin agus tá na daoine sin imithe le blianta agus múinteoirí maithe acu. Ní mórán cabhrach a thug an Eaglais dóibh – a mhalairt is baolach. Ach fé láthair tá Ráth Cairn go hiontach – tá foireann cantóirí agus ceoltóirí acu, bíonn caidreamh mór idir iad agus Gaeilgeoirí óga na Mí agus Bhaile Átha Cliath – siamsa acu féin – agus sórt éigin co-op, ag fás glasraí etc. Níor tháinig slua eile riamh arís, ach tá fo-dhuine a fuair talamh anseo is ansiúd ón nGaeltacht. Tá sé i gceist anois Comprehensive School do bhunú i Ráth Cairn mar mheánscoil Gaelach ar fad d'aon duine gur mian leo dul ann chomh maith le muintir Ráth Cairn agus Baile Ghib, agus an taisteal saor in aisce. Tá an-chuid as an dá áit gan amhras a fuair meánoideachas agus atá ag obair mar mhúinteoirí, banaltraí etc.

Tá roinnt is dócha i Sasana, ach ní níos mó ná as aon áit eile, agus tá an tríú glúin ag fás suas le Gaeilge – níl aon bhochtanas ann – nó náire orthu Gaeilge do labhairt.

An Ghaeilge ó shoin
Aguisín le Méadhbh

Is iomaí casadh ar staid na Gaeilge ó scríobh mo mháthair an t-alt sin. Léiríonn sí tuiscint ar na cúinsí a d'fhéadfadh bac a chur ar neart na Gaeilge ins na scoileanna, (an bhéim ar scríobh na Gaeilge seachas an chaint, agus dúnadh na gcolaistí ullmhúchain i 1960.) Ní dóigh liom gur tuigeadh di cé chomh mór is mar a rachadh na nithe sin i bhfeidhm ar obair na scoileanna. Bhí múinteoirí óga ag teacht ar an bhfód de réir a chéile gan taithí acu ar an nGaeilge mar mheán cumarsáide nádúrtha, gan taithí ar labhairt na teanga, agus gan an líofacht is gá chun teanga a sheachadadh go críochnúil. Ach tá an dearcadh dearfa san alt i gcoitinne a scríobhadh ins na luath-seascaidí. Bheadh Máirtín Ó Murchú ag teacht lei faoin tréimhse sin.

"Ba sa dara leath den fhichiú céad a thosaigh an toradh ar pholasaí Gaeilge an Stáit á fhoilsiú go soiléir." Sé sin an chéad abairt i gCuid a 3: *Cúlú* den phaimfléad *Ag dul ó Chion?* a d'fhoilsigh *An Aimsir Og* sa bhliain 2002. "Go híorónta, áfach, bhí iontaoibh an Stáit as an bpolasaí sin ag lagú faoin am sin."

Tá cuntas cuimsitheach sa phaimfléad ar *Cás na Gaeilge 1952-2002*, agus mar a chaill an Stát a mhisneach; mar a laghdaíodh stádas na Gaeilge ins na bunscoileanna; mar a cuireadh deireadh le "Gaeilge éigeantach" (1973); mar a deir Ó Murchú , "bhí na prapaí ba thábhachtaí dá raibh ag an Stát leis an teanga le leathchéad bliain i leataoibh agus ní raibh aon seasamh dáiríribh aici san Eoraip." Tá cúngú tagtha ar na ceantair ina bhfuil an Ghaeilge mar phríomhtheanga. Tháinig an teilifís agus meáin chumarsáide nach í chun tosaigh ins na seascaidí a bhí mar bheadh tsunami – tuile ag scuabadh chuile shórt roimpi idir shoineann agus dhoineann.

Ach tá ábhar dóchais ag teacht chun cinn ó shin. Ar cheann de ghnéithe suntasacha athbheochan na Gaeilge le blianta beaga anuas, tá fás leanúnach na nGaelscoileanna. In Éirinn agus i dTuaisceart Éireann araon in 2006 bhí beagnach 200 Gaelscoil, bunleibhéal agus iar-bhunleibhéal, lasmuigh den Ghaeltacht, i gcomparáid le 16 i 1972. Tharla athruithe tábhachtacha ar mheáin chumarsáide na Gaeilge le blianta beaga anuas chomh maith. Craolann RTÉ Raidió na Gaeltachta, seirbhís atá lonnaithe sa Ghaeltacht, 24 uaire in aghaidh an lae. Ó 1996 i leith, tá cainéal teilifíse Gaeilge, TG4 (Teilifís na Gaeilge ar dtús) ag craoladh. Tá nuachtán seachtainiúil, *Foinse*, lonnaithe i nGaeltacht na Gaillimhe agus foilsítear nuachtán laethúil, *Lá*, i mBéal Feirste. Bunaíodh comhlacht tras-teorann ar son na Gaeilge, Foras na Gaeilge, faoi Chomhaontú Aoine an Chéasta i 1998, agus tá cuid mhaith eagras deonach ag saothrú leo chomh maith. In 2003, ritheadh Acht na dTeangacha Oifigiúla, a thugann brí don chosaint bhunreachtúil atá ag an nGaeilge. De thoradh an Achta sin a bunaíodh Oifig an Choimisinéara Teanga (Gaeilge. ie) agus a baineadh amach stádas oifigiúil don Ghaeilge san Aontas Eorpach i 2005.

Lúnasa 2008